YOUR MESS,
GOD'S MIRACLE

STUDY GUIDE

Books by Samuel Rodriguez

Persevere with Power
Power for Your Day Devotional
Your Mess, God's Miracle

YOUR MESS, GOD'S MIRACLE

STUDY GUIDE

SAMUEL RODRIGUEZ

Chosen

a division of Baker Publishing Group
Minneapolis, Minnesota

Published by Chosen Books
Minneapolis, Minnesota
www.chosenbooks.com

Chosen Books is a division of
Baker Publishing Group, Grand Rapids, Michigan

Printed in the United States of America

ISBN 978-0-8007-6347-3 (trade paper)
ISBN 978-1-4934-4236-2 (ebook)

Cover design by Darren Welch Design

23 24 25 26 27 28 29   7 6 5 4 3 2 1

Contents

A Note from Pastor Sam   7

Getting Started   9

Session 1 Seeing Your Blind Spots   11

Session 2 Seeing the Power of Jesus   28

Session 3 Seeing the Miracle in Your Mess   44

Session 4 Seeing God's Spirit in Action   63

Session 5 Seeing What You've Never Seen Before   84

Session 6 Seeing Who You Are in Christ   106

Notes   125

A Note from Pastor Sam

How well you see often determines how well you live.

Your ability to see physically, intellectually and emotionally results from a multitude of variables, from genetics to educational opportunities, ocular health to empathy. Seeing spiritually, however, is available to anyone willing to place their faith in God by accepting the gift of salvation available through His Son, Jesus Christ. And how well you see spiritually determines whether you can look beyond the messy circumstances of life and glimpse God's miracles.

Spiritual vision doesn't rely on the accuracy of your eyes. Regardless of how well your pupils, irises and corneas work in harmony with your optic nerves, you can glimpse God's power, presence and purpose in your life and walk in faith by the power of the Holy Spirit. I realize this is easier to discuss in theological theory than to experience in rocky reality. Why? Because faith requires confidence in what usually cannot be seen by our human faculties: "Now faith is confidence in what we hope for and assurance about what we do not see" (Hebrews 11:1).

Too often, we allow the messiness of life to obstruct our spiritual vision and keep us focused on temporary trials rather than an eternal perspective. And like many people, you may often find your life filled with messes of one kind or another—chronic heartache and crushing debt, conflicted relationships and health struggles, depression and anxiety, addiction and despair. Overwhelmed by one blow after another and awaiting the next crisis or disappointment, you may feel your faith stretched to a breaking point. Rather than expecting a miracle, you're resigned to living in a continual mess, oblivious to the spiritual blinders limiting your ability to see what God wants to do in you and through you.

Which is why I find Jesus' encounter with the blind man described in John 9 to be so compelling, relevant and encouraging for us today. Jesus and His disciples were out walking and saw a man who had been blind from birth. The disciples asked about the cause of the man's congenital condition, and Jesus likely surprised them with His answer—and His actions. Spitting on the ground, He made mud with His saliva and the dirt, which He then spread over the blind man's eyes. Jesus then told the man, with his eyes still covered in this unexpected mud mask, to go wash himself in the nearby Pool of Siloam. The man went there, washed and returned *seeing*!

This encounter does more than describe a specific miracle during Jesus' time on earth. It offers us a stunning picture of how God often chooses to meet us in the muck and mire of our greatest challenges to produce a miracle of healing and wholeness. And that's what this study guide is all about!

As a companion to my book *Your Mess, God's Miracle*, this study can help you wash away the muddy messes in your life and open your eyes to your glorious future. God wants you to see clearly, and my prayer is that He will use these pages to open your eyes to His truth, even amid the messiness of where you may be right now. What Jesus did for the blind man is what He will do for you—if you're willing to trust Him through the mess. From the spit and mud of your life, get ready to discover His priceless gift and glimpse the miracle He's making!

Getting Started

As you'll discover throughout this study, seeing clearly and walking by faith go hand in hand. This study is designed to facilitate both, applying what you're learning as a way to draw closer to God and to experience more of the Holy Spirit's power in your life. Whether you're going through this study in community with a group or individually as a way to grow in your faith, you're likely to benefit most by engaging the content with an open mind and tender heart.

Each session contains two major sections. The first explores the major themes and biblical truths found in corresponding chapters of *Your Mess, God's Miracle* and works well for groups as well as individual study. The second, "Look Again," takes you deeper into the material, offering opportunities for reflection and personal application. If you're in a group, this second section provides a great way to continue processing what you're learning in between your group meetings.

Both sections include passages from the Bible, all from the NIV unless noted otherwise. Both sections also contain lots of questions to help you explore the material, but don't feel like you have to use them all. Groups can focus on the questions and exercises that resonate with participants most. Individuals completing this study can ask God's Spirit to guide them to truths especially relevant to where they are in their spiritual journey.

Keep in mind that none of the components of this study are intended to burden you with homework or leave you feeling obligated to do more. Instead, remain open to the ways this study can enhance your understanding of *Your Mess, God's Miracle* and draw you deeper into your relationship with Christ. You're encouraged to respond in the spaces provided throughout these pages. While you don't have to write down your responses, you might be surprised to discover how jotting them down helps focus your thoughts.

Finally, remember that all this is an opportunity to explore new ways of considering what it means to clarify your spiritual sight and gain a fresh perspective as you grow and mature in your faith. Ultimately, this study is intended to kick-start your mind and heart so you're inspired to keep your eyes focused on Jesus, following His example and experiencing the freedom that comes from living out your identity in Him. Are you ready to see what you've never seen before? Then it's time to look beyond your mess and discover God's miracle!

SESSION 1

Seeing Your Blind Spots

Our God is not only the God who restores.
Our God is a God who gives us what we have never had before!
Your Mess, God's Miracle, chapter 1, page 15

So we fix our eyes not on what is seen, but on what is unseen, since what is seen is temporary, but what is unseen is eternal.
2 Corinthians 4:18

Open Your Eyes

We all have blind spots.

Literally, our eyes have a small spot at the back of each retina where the optic nerve enters the eyeball. This circular area has no rods and cones and shows no sensitivity to light.[1] Even people with 20/20 vision have these blind spots.

Metaphorically, blind spots refer to anything we're unable to see within a certain field of vision and perspective. Drivers and cyclists learn that even with rearview mirrors and cameras, they might not see certain obstacles near them. Investors know that regardless of how much information they collect about a company before investing, certain unknown risks remain. And we rarely see ourselves and others accurately but instead selectively focus on certain aspects, both positive and negative.

Spiritually, we all have blind spots, too. These are often vulnerable areas of weakness that go undefended and unguarded until we face temptation and give in. We may not realize how much we idolize something or someone until we've grown overly dependent on them. Spiritual blind spots can also result from sinful struggles with pride, self-righteousness, entitlement, anger, jealousy, envy or fear. Any time you lose sight of God, the devil tries to blindfold you and keep you from seeing the truth.

For example, you may want to grow closer to God by praying each day, but you tell yourself you simply don't have enough time to pray regularly. The truth that you're evading, however, is that you spend wasted hours surfing social media each day. You're aware that if you took an inventory of how you spend your day, you could easily find time to pray. But staying busy and distracted, which social media facilitates, prevents you from following through and doing what you truly long to do. The enemy does all he can to reinforce this blind spot so that you won't focus more time and attention on God.

Denial and diversion are also powerful tactics that prevent us from seeing clearly. When we don't like looking at areas that make us feel uncomfortable, ashamed and aware of our sinfulness, we often try to turn away and ignore them. Over time, these blind spots grow larger as our spiritual vision grows blurry and we drift into darkness. When we don't see clearly, we're more likely to focus less on God and more on ourselves.

The encounter between Jesus and the blind man in John 9 reminds us that in order to see, we must examine our blind spots and keep our focus on Christ. We need to acknowledge our blind spots so we can see how essential it is to rely on God to fully restore our vision. We all need the miraculous healing power of Jesus in our lives if we're to dispel the darkness and live in the light of His truth.

- What comes to mind when you think of various blind spots in your life? When has a blind spot left you vulnerable to danger or conflict?

- What's one area of your life that you would like to see more clearly and accurately? What impairs or obstructs your ability to see this particular area the way God sees it?

Focus Your Vision

The following passage from God's Word anchors this entire study, so read it slowly. If in a group, you might invite someone to read it aloud as everyone follows along. Look for fresh insight as you consider the scene described here and then answer the questions that follow.

> As he went along, he saw a man blind from birth. His disciples asked him, "Rabbi, who sinned, this man or his parents, that he was born blind?"
>
> "Neither this man nor his parents sinned," said Jesus, "but this happened so that the works of God might be displayed in him. As long as it is day, we must do the works of him who sent me. Night is coming, when no one can work. While I am in the world, I am the light of the world."
>
> After saying this, he spit on the ground, made some mud with the saliva, and put it on the man's eyes. "Go," he told him, "wash in the Pool of Siloam" (this word means "Sent"). So the man went and washed, and came home seeing.
>
> John 9:1–7

- Why do you suppose the disciples immediately assumed that sin, either his own or his parents', caused this man's blindness?

- How does Jesus' response to the disciples provide a new way of considering the blind man's condition and the cause of it? Does His response surprise you? Why or why not?

- Have you ever considered that your problems, limitations and struggles occur so that the works of God might be displayed in you and your life? When have you experienced God's miraculous presence and power in the midst of a recent challenge?

- Out of all the ways Jesus could have chosen to heal the blind man, why do you suppose He chose to spit on the ground, make mud and apply it to the man's eyes?

Seeing Is Believing

You've probably endured times when you felt in the dark, unable to see your way forward. Your darkness might have been caused by unexpected circumstances or painful discoveries. It might have resulted from battling a disease, recovering from an injury, losing your job, ending a relationship or moving to a new home. Even when experiencing blessings and God's favor, you may sometimes feel a bit disoriented about how to move forward once you're down from the mountaintop.

Just as sight requires many components working together, the kind of darkness that leads to spiritual blindness has many shades. In fact, you may not realize how the shadows have been closing in on you until you need the light. Sometimes the worst kind of blindness progressively escapes your awareness until you can no longer see clearly. In order to live in the light of God's divine love and experience the power of the Holy Spirit in your life, you must be willing to open your eyes to the power of Christ's healing touch.

Because no matter how well things may be going or how strong your faith, you can never see everything going on the way God does. Some events may blindside you so suddenly and unexpectedly that your world turns upside down. Other kinds of blindness may result from your unwillingness to see what is right in front of you. Whether it is out of fear, uncertainty, denial or an attempt to control your life, you choose to ignore the log in your own eye while pointing out specks in the eyes of others (Matthew 7:5).

Even after you have invited Jesus into your life as your Lord and Savior and have welcomed the Holy Spirit into your heart, you may still experience momentary blindness. Times when you refuse to obey God's Word in order to justify giving in to temptation. Moments when you tell yourself there are no consequences for the secrets you keep. Seasons when you can't see how far you're drifting away from God when you stop going to church. When you hang out with people who encourage you to do things you know God doesn't want you to do. When you turn to old habits and addictions to numb the pain of life's trials and traumas. When you ignore consequences—at work, at home, at school, at church—until they cannot be ignored.

But no matter how dark your situation, there is always hope through the power of Jesus Christ. The blind man's eyes had not worked properly since birth, which left him resigned to never experiencing sight. Without being able to see anything for his entire life, he likely never expected to receive something he had never had.

But Jesus made it clear to His disciples: "Neither this man nor his parents sinned . . . but this happened so that the works of God might be displayed in him" (John 9:3). The blind man's condition was not a punishment or even the consequence of anyone's sin—it was an opportunity for God's power, glory and goodness to produce a miracle.

So no matter what you're facing—blindness, cancer, bankruptcy, divorce, addiction, homelessness, betrayal—nothing is impossible for God! What you perceive as impossible is simply an inaccurate perception based on your human limitations. Jesus Himself said, "With man this is impossible, but with God all things are possible" (Matthew 19:26). When you have the power of the Holy Spirit within you, then you can move mountains with faith as small as a mustard seed (Matthew 17:20)!

- What problems, limitations or burdens have you carried for such a long time that you've resigned yourself to their permanence in your life? How have they affected your relationship with God?

- What resonates most for you in the way Jesus healed the blind man? Why?

- When have you experienced a time of darkness when you struggled to see yourself, your life and God clearly? How did you move forward when you couldn't see which way to go?

- What current struggles are affecting your ability to see with spiritual clarity? What's required for you to experience God's presence and power in the midst of these messes?

Miracle in Your Mess

Pause for a moment and consider what it means to be enveloped by darkness. If possible, turn off or dim the lights where you are right now and then close your eyes for at least sixty seconds. Still your heart before God and think about what it means to experience the illuminating light of Christ in your life at this time.

- How would you describe your experience in darkness just now? What did you feel as you closed your eyes and sat in the dark?

- When have you struggled to see clearly and felt in the dark about what you should do? What has helped you in the past to decide your next steps during these times?

Keep in mind that seeing clearly beyond your messes to glimpse God's miracles usually takes time. The apostle Paul reminds us, "Now we see things imperfectly, like puzzling reflections in a mirror, but then we will see everything with perfect clarity. All that I know now is partial and incomplete, but then I will know everything completely, just as God now knows me completely" (1 Corinthians 13:12 NLT).

In this first section, you've started exploring what it means to recognize blind spots and areas of darkness in your life in order to embrace the power Christ has made available to you. Taking note of where you are spiritually is a good way to begin. Toward this goal, spend a few minutes answering the following questions in the space provided. Remember, no one will see your responses unless you choose to share them.

- What stands out for you in this first section? What words or phrases linger in your mind and heart at this time?

- As you consider what it means to see your blind spots, what concerns or fears come to mind? What are your areas of weakness right now?

- Finally, what are your expectations for this study? How can the message in *Your Mess, God's Miracle* help you to grow in your faith and draw closer to God?

Review your answers and ask God to meet you right where you are. Spend a few minutes in prayer, thanking God for how He is already at work in your life. Ask Him to use this study to help you see clearly so you can dispel darkness and experience the joy, peace and purpose He has for you. Trust that He is on the move and birthing a miracle in the midst of each messy area of your life.

—— LOOK AGAIN ——

Just because you cannot imagine your miracle does not mean that God's power is not already in the midst of your mud. Just because there is mud in your eyes right now does not mean that you are not about to receive new vision.

Your Mess, God's Miracle, chapter 2, page 46

In this section, you are invited to further explore how you can see clearly and experience more power through the Holy Spirit as you discover God's miracle in the midst of your mess. The questions and exercises below are intended to be more personal in nature as you process all you're learning and apply it to your life. If you're completing this study in a group, "Look Again" provides individual opportunities to continue your momentum at a deeper level. While you're certainly encouraged to share findings with your group as the Spirit leads, keep in mind the primary emphasis in this section is on strengthening your personal relationship with God.

First, you'll take a moment to **See the Light** as you read a passage of Scripture that relates to the big ideas in the previous section and reflect on its relevance to your messy, miraculous journey. This is an opportunity to meditate on God's Word as you become more attuned to the whisper of His Spirit in your heart. Next, you will encounter a **Fresh Perspective** as you personalize God's message and spend some time with Him in prayer. Finally, you will take practical action steps to implement all you're learning as you begin to **Watch Where You're Going**. These exercises require you to take small risks that can reap big rewards in how you see yourself, others and God.

Before beginning, you will want to have read chapters 1 and 2 in *Your Mess, God's Miracle*. Feel free to answer and respond in the spaces provided below or use a journal or notebook to keep all your responses and exercises related to this study together in one place. You don't have to answer all of the prompts, but you may find this personal study more effective if you engage with all three sections.

See the Light

When you see with your eyes, light provides illumination so you can discern shapes, sizes, textures, dimensions and distances. When you see with the eyes of your heart, God's Word provides illumination so you can grow in wisdom, discernment, truth, obedience and character. Your prayers join with the psalmist's as you spend time in the Bible and begin to see more clearly: "Your word is a lamp for my feet, a light on my path" (Psalm 119:105).

In our world today, subjective standards have become the norm, allowing individuals and groups to redefine truth, sometimes daily, based on subjective perspectives, social trends and personal whims. Which is why spending time in God's Word—studying and meditating and listening—is vital to your spiritual vision and maturity. The Bible provides the unchanging lens of God's truth, which is consistent, reliable and illuminating for your life. It has divine power to infuse your vision with supernatural insight and an eternal perspective. We're told "For the word of God is alive and active. Sharper than any double-edged sword, it penetrates even to dividing soul and spirit, joints and marrow; it judges the thoughts and attitudes of the heart" (Hebrews 4:12).

To help bring more of God's light into the way you see things, read Psalm 139 below, then use the questions that follow to aid in your reflection on how it applies to your life:

> You have searched me, LORD,
>   and you know me.
> You know when I sit and when I rise;
>   you perceive my thoughts from afar.
> You discern my going out and my lying down;
>   you are familiar with all my ways.
> Before a word is on my tongue
>   you, LORD, know it completely.
> You hem me in behind and before,
>   and you lay your hand upon me.
> Such knowledge is too wonderful for me,
>   too lofty for me to attain.
>
> Where can I go from your Spirit?
>   Where can I flee from your presence?

If I go up to the heavens, you are there;
    if I make my bed in the depths, you are there.
If I rise on the wings of the dawn,
    if I settle on the far side of the sea,
even there your hand will guide me,
    your right hand will hold me fast.
If I say, "Surely the darkness will hide me
    and the light become night around me,"
even the darkness will not be dark to you;
    the night will shine like the day,
    for darkness is as light to you.

For you created my inmost being;
    you knit me together in my mother's womb.
I praise you because I am fearfully and wonderfully made;
    your works are wonderful,
    I know that full well.
My frame was not hidden from you
    when I was made in the secret place,
    when I was woven together in the depths of the earth.
Your eyes saw my unformed body;
    all the days ordained for me were written in your book
    before one of them came to be.
How precious to me are your thoughts, God!
    How vast is the sum of them!
Were I to count them,
    they would outnumber the grains of sand—
    when I awake, I am still with you.

If only you, God, would slay the wicked!
    Away from me, you who are bloodthirsty!
They speak of you with evil intent;
    your adversaries misuse your name.
Do I not hate those who hate you, LORD,
    and abhor those who are in rebellion against you?
I have nothing but hatred for them;
    I count them my enemies.
Search me, God, and know my heart;
    test me and know my anxious thoughts.

See if there is any offensive way in me,
and lead me in the way everlasting.

Psalm 139

- Read through this psalm again, this time circling or underlining the words and phrases that resonate most with you. Now go back and look at what you've pulled out. How do these words and phrases speak to your life presently? What might God be saying to you through them?

- What does it mean to you that nothing can separate you from God's Spirit? How does the light of His love ensure that you will never be permanently in darkness?

- How does the knowledge that you are "fearfully and wonderfully made" (verse 14) affect the way you see your life? Your relationship with others? With God?

- How can praying this psalm help you identify your blind spots and invite God's illuminating presence?

Fresh Perspective

It's not easy in the midst of life's messes to see God's hand at work mixing a miracle from the mud. When Jesus spit on the ground, rubbed His saliva into the dirt and then used the just-made mud to mask the blind man's eyes, those present—including the blind man himself—were likely confused. *What in the world could Jesus be up to?* the disciples might have wondered. *Why is this stranger placing mud, which He just made by the sound of it, over my sightless eyes?* the blind man might have thought.

We can't know the full extent of Jesus' motive in using such unexpected means to heal this man who had been blind from birth, but we can believe with confidence that His method remains relevant for our lives today. Christ's holy and perfect DNA contained in the saliva He used to mix mud from the dirty, dusty ground produced the essence of a miracle the blind man likely never expected. In many ways, this mixture reflects the essence of the incarnation, of the Word made flesh. The fact that God sent His only beloved Son to be born and live as a man testifies to this same meeting of heaven and earth.

Even though you cannot see it with your earthly eyes, Jesus remains present in the daily details of your life. Through the power of His Spirit dwelling in you, a transformation is taking place at this very moment. Areas of darkness and blindness will soon be dispelled as you wash away the mud from your eyes and focus on Jesus. There will still be pain and suffering at times, but there will also be a fuller awareness of your heavenly Father's power, joy and purpose at work in your life. This is the kind of perspective James describes:

> Consider it pure joy, my brothers and sisters, whenever you face trials of many kinds, because you know that the testing of your faith produces perseverance. Let perseverance finish its work so that you may be mature and complete, not lacking anything. If any of you lacks wisdom, you should ask God, who gives generously to all without finding fault, and it will be given to you.
>
> James 1:2–5

- What does it mean to "consider it pure joy" in the midst of the trials you're facing? According to James, what's the basis for experiencing joy in the midst of suffering?

- What are some of the blessings that have emerged from hard times in the past? When have you looked back and realized God redeemed a past wound into a reflection of His glory?

- What present trial, temptation, disappointment or suffering is impeding your spiritual vision? What accompanying emotions—fear, anxiety, anger or depression, to name a few—may be compounding this struggle?

- Considered another way, what is your greatest blind spot that needs God's power, protection and provision? What glimpses have you caught that your Master is mixing mud into a miracle in the midst of this challenging time?

Watch Where You're Going

One of the advantages of being part of the body of Christ is having others see what you can't see. Confiding in trusted believers allows them to offer their perspectives, share your burdens and encourage you to persevere in the midst of your toughest times. God never intended for us to live independently and self-sufficiently as we follow Jesus and walk by faith. He wants us in relationships that facilitate truth and clarity so we can help one another know Him, love Him and serve Him more.

To begin seeing more clearly, make an appointment in the next few days with a believer you know and trust. It could be a friend from church, someone in your small group, a neighbor whose faith you admire or a fellow pilgrim who is also reading *Your Mess, God's Miracle* and completing this study. Set up a time to meet at a place where you won't be distracted or interrupted for at least an hour.

During this time, confide in this person regarding one area of struggle that's preventing you from seeing yourself and God clearly. After sharing what you've been learning about blind spots in your life, use the prompts below to facilitate your conversation.

My biggest blind spot right now is _____,
and it's hindering my spiritual growth because _____
_____.

I want to believe God's at work producing a miracle in my mess, but I struggle because _____

_____ .

What do you see in my life that may also be getting in the way of my relationship with God?

When have you witnessed God's miraculous power at work in the messes of your own life? What have you learned about being patient and trusting Him in the process?

What truth from God's Word has given you hope and sustained you in the midst of your trials and struggles?

Before you wrap up, ask this individual to pray for you in the days to come. Thank them for the encouragement they've offered, and if possible, arrange to meet with them again before you complete this study. After your meeting, spend some time reflecting on what they shared and how God might be speaking through them to help you see more clearly.

Seeing the Power of Jesus

Jesus heals our vision—our ability to see our sin, our need and God's grace—even when we do not realize that we are blind.

Your Mess, God's Miracle, chapter 2, page 40

It is because of him that you are in Christ Jesus, who has become for us wisdom from God—that is, our righteousness, holiness and redemption.

1 Corinthians 1:30

Open Your Eyes

Most people don't enjoy being seen in their messiness. Whether it's the literal, tangible clutter and chaos of a disorganized and neglected area or the emotional mess miring us in our pain, our shame, our seemingly uncontrollable habits and addictions, exposing our messiness feels like we're only making matters worse. We may feel revealed to be less than the put-together person we present on social media. We fear that if others saw the messes we're hiding they would judge, reject and abandon us.

You may have noticed that your messiness also causes distress, internal conflict, frustration and confusion. According to many neurologists and psychologists, human brains are wired to analyze and organize all the incoming sensory data and sort it into manageable groupings, patterns and conclusions.[1] Such mental organization helps us compare the similarities and differences around us, whether in people or our environment, as well as in us, with our various thoughts, emotions, memories and physical reactions. When we encounter something that doesn't quite fit or causes us pain or discomfort, we naturally pause to reclassify it, find a place for it or compartmentalize and ignore it.

This strategy works for keeping the junk drawers in our kitchens closed, but not so well when it comes to the collections of stuffed emotions and experiences we keep hidden inside us. When we struggle with sinful secrets, harmful habits and unhealthy relationships that go against what we know is right, what we know God has told us to do, then we experience distress. Which, unfortunately, often sends us running for the temporary comfort and mild alleviation those illicit attachments seem to provide. Our messiness inside feels like a swirling cycle without any way for us to break the riptide pulling us under, drawing us away from God and from who He made us to be.

This personal, internal kind of messiness often leaves us feeling hopeless and desperate. Messy rooms can be decluttered, sorted, tidied and cleaned. Messy hearts, conversations and relationships, however, often require more than we can muster. They require experiencing the power of Jesus to help us see clearly, encounter cleansing and make room for God's miracle.

- What's the messiest room or area in your home right now? What items and factors contribute to its mess?

- What's the messiest issue or struggle you're facing internally right now? What has spilled and sprawled inside your heart to contribute to this mess?

Focus Your Vision

Jesus didn't have to use the messy manner He chose to gift the blind man with a miracle. Because we know nothing is accidental with God, we can assume Jesus definitely had His reasons, perhaps foremost to illustrate His power to bless our mess into wholeness even when we—like the man blind since birth—cannot see the extent of our mess clearly. Thankfully for us, Jesus heals our vision—our ability to see our sin, our need and God's grace—even when we don't realize we're blind!

We find this kind of healing encounter in another intriguing scene—when Jesus faced a woman exposed in a compromising, humiliating situation. Slowly read the following passage describing this encounter; if you're part of a group study, you might ask someone to read it aloud while everyone else follows along. Compare this scene to Jesus' encounter with the blind man and then answer the questions that follow.

Jesus returned to the Mount of Olives, but early the next morning he was back again at the Temple. A crowd soon gathered, and he sat down and taught them. As he was speaking, the teachers of religious law and the Pharisees brought a woman who had been caught in the act of adultery. They put her in front of the crowd.

"Teacher," they said to Jesus, "this woman was caught in the act of adultery. The law of Moses says to stone her. What do you say?"

They were trying to trap him into saying something they could use against him, but Jesus stooped down and wrote in the dust with his finger. They kept demanding an answer, so he stood up again and said, "All right, but let the one who has never sinned throw the first stone!" Then he stooped down again and wrote in the dust.

When the accusers heard this, they slipped away one by one, beginning with the oldest, until only Jesus was left in the middle of the crowd with the woman. Then Jesus stood up again and said to the woman, "Where are your accusers? Didn't even one of them condemn you?"

"No, Lord," she said.

And Jesus said, "Neither do I. Go and sin no more."

John 8:1–11 NLT

- Does Jesus' response to the religious leaders surprise you? Why or why not?

- Just as Jesus used dirt to make mud that healed the blind man, here He writes in the dusty ground. Why do you suppose Jesus writes on the ground to convey His message to the Pharisees and religious leaders rather than speaking to them?

- What do you imagine Jesus wrote on the ground that caused the religious leaders to slip away one by one? What do you think motivated their departure after they had been so zealous to trap Jesus?

- How does Jesus' response to the accused woman display both respect for the Law of Moses and, more importantly, the grace of God?

Seeing Is Believing

Jesus displayed both compassion and authority with the woman caught in adultery. Keep in mind her accusers considered her not only a criminal, but also so unclean as to be punished by death at the hands of those who rigorously followed Jewish laws. She had violated laws that were cultural and moral as well as religious.

Can you imagine the utter shame and embarrassment she endured? Since no mention is made, we might assume that her partner in crime, the man with whom she had been caught, was not held to the same standard as this woman. But there she was, literally and figuratively naked in her sin, when the religious leaders barged in and forcefully dragged her to the temple, where Jesus was teaching. Surely few moments in her life were as degrading and shameful as those when she was used as bait by the Jewish leaders hoping to trap Jesus in their legalism.

Jesus, however, obviously knew better. He understood exactly what these religious leaders were up to with such a bold display. Ironically, they presented this woman whom they found in the act of adultery as a brazen example of breaking the law that God had given to Moses. Yet they themselves were just as guilty in their own sins of judgment, condemnation and hypocrisy.

And perhaps that's how Jesus allowed the Pharisees' trap to backfire on them. We don't know what He wrote in the dusty ground. Perhaps it was a verse or phrase from the ancient Scriptures challenging their condemnation. Christ's finger-scrawled message might have been a list of the sins committed in private by the leaders themselves. While we can't know specifically what the Master wrote, we know the result it had. One by one, the accusers slipped away, likely with a sense of their own shame and humiliation.

In this encounter, God's message is clear:

> There is no one righteous, not even one;
>> there is no one who understands;
>> there is no one who seeks God.
> All have turned away,
>> they have together become worthless;
> there is no one who does good,
>> not even one.
>
> Romans 3:10–12;
> see also Psalm 14:1–3

Jesus did not accuse this woman brought before Him, although clearly, she had broken the Law. He told her to go on her way, to recognize her sin and to no longer be who she had been. He helped her to see herself, her mess and God in a way that was radically different from how the Pharisees did. Jesus restored her sight to see her messy life was not too big for the Master's miracle.

- When have you been caught or seen in the midst of a sinful situation? How would you describe your experience looking back on it now?

- What speaks to you personally about the way Jesus regarded the woman caught in adultery? Why?

- When have you experienced the judgment and condemnation of others in the midst of your struggle? How did you experience God's grace despite their disapproval?

- What sinful habits or ongoing struggles might be obscuring your vision of yourself, your need and God? How can you invite the power of Jesus into those challenges?

Miracle in Your Mess

The blind man had no reason to expect that he would be given the gift of sight on the day Jesus placed mud over his eyes. The woman caught in adultery likely expected to be condemned to death, terrified and alone, when the Jewish leaders literally dragged her from her lover's bed to the temple, where Jesus was teaching. Most likely, neither of these individuals—the blind man and the woman caught in adultery—dared to hope for the miracle they received.

But you should.

While you may not be expecting to see what God's about to do in your life, that doesn't mean you shouldn't dare to hope and be ready to receive what the Lord has for you. Considering how Jesus poured His power into those He healed and encountered, you should expect to be surprised! If you're serious about wanting to invite Jesus into your mess so that He can bless it and transform it into His miracle, then get ready.

Get ready to see what you have never seen before.

Get ready to hope for what your heart has never dared to hope for before.

Get ready to receive the miracle you need most from the One who knows you best.

Personally, professionally, privately and publicly—through the miraculous power of Jesus Christ, you are about to experience God's miracle in your mess.

The power of Jesus can heal, transform, illuminate and redeem your messes in ways you cannot even imagine. In fact, in the Bible God promises to exceed your human capacity to imagine what He can and will do in your life: "But, as it is written, 'What no eye has seen, nor ear heard, nor the heart of man imagined, what God has prepared for those who love him'" (1 Corinthians 2:9 ESV). This promise applies to what awaits you in heaven as well as the miracle God is working for you here on earth.

- What expectations do you have for experiencing God's miracle in your personal messes? Are you more afraid to hope because you might be disappointed, or are you more afraid to be surprised by the power of Jesus in your life?

- What miracle would you most like to experience in a messy area of your life? As you imagine it, what might this miracle look like?

- How has God surprised you in miraculous ways in the past? How has He surprised you the most up until now?

- What specifically do you need the power of Jesus to do in your life right now? What can God do in your messiness that you simply cannot?

--- **LOOK AGAIN** ---

When you encounter the sight-giving, life-changing and heart-transforming power of Jesus, you are no longer who you once were.

Your Mess, God's Miracle, chapter 3, page 57

As you continue exploring more of God's power in your life, use the questions and exercises below to help you personalize your application and implementation. Remember, if you're completing this study in a group, this "Look Again" section is intended to facilitate your individual study as you grow closer to the Lord and stronger in your faith.

As with the previous session, you will likely find it helpful to have read chapters 2 and 3 in *Your Mess, God's Miracle* before completing what follows. You're free to answer and respond in the spaces provided below or use a journal or notebook for all your responses and exercises related to this study. It's okay if you don't answer all of the questions here, but you may find this personal process more engaging if you explore all three sections.

See the Light

What comes to mind when you think of power in your everyday life? You probably have electric power that's wired into your home so you can enjoy the many conveniences—ovens, microwaves, dishwashers, washers and dryers—that are often taken for granted in our technology-enveloped world. Phones, laptops and tablets require power as well, whether from electricity or batteries. The cars you drive and the transportation you use require power, too, whether they have gas-fueled or electric engines.

You may think of power as more of an abstract quality held by military units, law enforcement and political authorities. This kind of power relies on establishing laws, punishing offenders and controlling chaos to achieve a certain status quo. Such social, cultural and political power is wielded in the way organizations report facts and respond to criticism, whether in person or through social media.

Power also refers to both physical strength and internal fortitude. People who train their bodies increase their physical power by gaining muscle mass through workouts and repetitions. If you've ever battled disease, illness or injury, you know the power to persevere connects the power of your body with the power of your mind, heart and emotions. You use power to push through certain limitations and obstacles to achieve your goals, whether for healing or completing work.

God's power, however, is the most potent kind of power on earth. Why? Because it has no limits or constraints. Jesus told His followers, "With man this is impossible, but with God all things are possible" (Matthew 19:26). So often you may feel anxious, worried or frustrated because you've done all you know to do. Once you reach the end of your resources, you struggle to imagine what else can be done. Thankfully for us, God is never limited by our imaginations' inability to envision the miracle we so desperately need.

The Psalms address the infinite, limitless power of God by finding poetic and metaphorical ways to describe what ultimately defies human description. Read through the passage below from Psalm 147 and then answer the questions that follow.

> The Lord builds up Jerusalem;
>   he gathers the exiles of Israel.
> He heals the brokenhearted
>   and binds up their wounds.
> He determines the number of the stars
>   and calls them each by name.
> Great is our Lord and mighty in power;
>   his understanding has no limit.
> The Lord sustains the humble
>   but casts the wicked to the ground.
>
> Sing to the Lord with grateful praise;
>   make music to our God on the harp.
>
> He covers the sky with clouds;
>   he supplies the earth with rain
>   and makes grass grow on the hills.
> He provides food for the cattle
>   and for the young ravens when they call.

His pleasure is not in the strength of the horse,
　　nor his delight in the legs of the warrior;
the LORD delights in those who fear him,
　　who put their hope in his unfailing love.

Psalm 147:2–11

- What attributes of God reflect His power, according to this passage? What are some ways God's power is depicted here?

- With such immense, limitless strength, why does God not delight in His power for its own sake? Why does He delight instead in those who fear Him?

- God's power is seen in a variety of endeavors in these verses. How does His power influence His creation? His protection of us? His provision for us?

- What words, phrases or images resonate most with you in this passage? Why do you suppose they stand out to you?

Fresh Perspective

Often when you're struggling, it may feel difficult—perhaps even impossible—to imagine how God can meet you and work in your life. When your relationships explode, your support systems disappear and your emotions overwhelm you, you may believe the only miracle possible is for God to solve your problems, reconcile your relationships and take away your pain.

But what if God meets you in the midst of all that messiness? What if His miracle doesn't look the way you expect it to look? What if it takes longer than you feel like it should? What if He's making mud from your mess in order to give you something you could not receive otherwise?

No matter what your mess looks like, no matter how much pain you're experiencing, no matter how unsettled and chaotic your life might seem, Jesus has the power to restore, recharge and redeem all the jagged, messy parts and broken pieces. When you allow Him to make mud from the ground below your feet, you accept that you may not be able to see exactly what He's doing in the moment.

Remember, the blind man exercised faith by not questioning or resisting the strange action made by a virtual stranger. He participated by allowing Jesus into the darkness of his sightless world. Often you may struggle to see how God is moving and where He is taking you. But even when your inability to see clearly leads to doubt and fear and uncertainty, you step out in faith, trusting that Christ equips and empowers you for your journey. That His power is sufficient.

The apostle Paul shared about his experience in accessing the power of Jesus in a letter to believers in the early Church at Corinth. After battling what he described as a "thorn in my flesh" (2 Corinthians 12:7), Paul prayed for God to remove it three times before receiving an answer that likely wasn't what he expected:

> Three times I pleaded with the Lord to take it away from me. But he said to me, "My grace is sufficient for you, for my power is made perfect in weakness." Therefore I will boast all the more gladly about my weaknesses, so that Christ's power may rest on me. That is why, for Christ's sake, I delight in weaknesses, in insults, in hardships, in persecutions, in difficulties. For when I am weak, then I am strong.
>
> 2 Corinthians 12:8–10

As you become more aware of your blindness, of your life's messiness, of your limitations, you need not despair. According to Paul, such a vulnerable position allows you to experience Christ's power in your life with renewed intensity. What you see and feel as your weakness and inability to overcome obstacles is actually the beginning of a new clarity, freedom and strength.

Spend some time in prayer, at least ten minutes, and ask God to meet you in your weakness, in your brokenness, in your messiness. Use this prayer-starter to help you begin your conversation, but open your heart and make it your own.

Dear Jesus, I need Your healing, miraculous resurrection power in my life right now. So much of life feels messy and complicated. I struggle and struggle and find myself getting stuck in the same old patterns, habits and ruts. In order to break free and see clearly, I surrender all I am to You, Lord. Meet me right here, right now. Mix Your divine power with the muddy mess of my challenges. Fill me with Your Holy Spirit so that I might receive a fresh burst of heavenly power. Thank You, Jesus, for being more than sufficient for all my needs, all my messes. Amen.

Watch Where You're Going

Many times when you feel mired in a mess, you experience a sense of chaos and disorder both within and around yourself. To what extent your internal messiness influences your messy environment, or vice versa, may be hard to distinguish. Some experts would say they go hand in hand.

In her bestselling book *Outer Order, Inner Calm*, Gretchen Rubin explores this correlation between one's internal distress from emotional clutter and the external disorder sprawling in one's environment. "Our rooms shape our thoughts, and our possessions change our moods," she writes. "It can be challenging to influence our thoughts and actions directly; by improving the state of our surroundings, we can improve our state of mind."[2]

The relationship between what you experience internally and externally is biblical as well. God's Word says, "By wisdom a house is built, and through understanding it is established; through knowledge its rooms are filled with rare and beautiful treasures" (Proverbs 24:3–4). Wisdom, understanding and knowledge help construct houses that are well-established and filled with unique treasures. While this passage relies on a metaphor, it implies that how we deal with our internal messes is often reflected in how we handle our external ones.

Whether you agree with this correlation or not, choose a messy area in your home or office to sort and reorder. Choose something that's primarily your mess and not someone else's. You will also want to keep your target area small enough to tackle in less than an hour. But you may be surprised what you can accomplish when you focus on bringing order and organization to a specific place.

You might clean out a junk drawer in your home that's become a catch-all for various disparate items. Perhaps a kitchen cupboard overflowing with spices and utensils needs purging and reorganizing. It could be the clutter covering your desk space or dining room table, a shelf in your bathroom crammed with assorted toiletry items or a hall closet bulging with years' worth of collected possessions.

So set your phone or smart-watch alarm for one hour and try to stay focused on what this one area needs for order and cleanliness to be restored. After your hour is up or your goal is complete, answer the following questions.

- What was the most challenging aspect of cleaning up this messy area? How did you overcome this challenge?

- What did you enjoy most about tackling this messy space and restoring order in it? What felt satisfying about completing this task?

- How would you describe your internal experience of restoring external order to this contained area? To what would you compare it?

- Based on your experience, do you agree that your environment often reflects your heart's condition? Why or why not?

SESSION 3

Seeing the Miracle in Your Mess

When we look for power, purpose and peace in anything other than God, we underestimate all that He has for us.

Your Mess, God's Miracle, chapter 3, page 67

Now faith is confidence in what we hope for and assurance about what we do not see.

Hebrews 11:1

Open Your Eyes

When was the last time you lost or misplaced something only to realize it was right in front of you? Like most people, you've likely endured frantic searches for keys, glasses, phones or wallets, and then looked in your pocket, on your face, next to your chair or in your bag to find the elusive item. It was there the entire time you were searching, but you failed to see it even as your eyes scanned it.

You may get so busy and distracted bouncing from one urgent demand to another each day that you lose sight of what your eyes are seeing. You get into a cycle of home responsibilities, work responsibilities and family and community responsibilities, and your life feels like it's passing you by. You're running on autopilot, going through the motions of what's required of you but failing to engage with the people, moments and events you encounter daily.

When you're caught up in one of these seasons, it's often even harder to see what's going on in your life spiritually. Part of losing focus is the result of no longer praying, reading the Word, serving others or spending time listening to God. But another factor obscuring your spiritual vision is often conditional living, waiting on a day when you'll have more time for God, when you will be better able to focus clearly on Him and what He's doing in your life. Meanwhile, you run and race from place to place, seeing but not seeing what matters most.

When you miss out on seeing what you have and what you need in the present because you're living conditionally in the future, you often tighten the blindfold you're wearing. You assume you will experience more power, peace, joy and purpose someday when you're more spiritually mature or at some future date when God blesses you with what your heart longs to receive. Until then, you may feel like there's nothing much you can do other than wait. Like the man blind since birth, you don't even realize how seeing clearly can change your life.

The problem, however, is that you may need to shift your perspective. Rather than looking out the wrong end of your life's telescope and seeing only yourself, you need to turn your lens around and look up. While you're waiting on God to show you the next steps for your life, He is waiting on you to see what's already in front of you, accessible right now. Instead of waiting on God to move in your life, to answer your prayers, to make His will clear for your life, He is already present with you and trying to get your attention.

One of the ways God often gets our attention is through our pain. When life doesn't work the way we hope or expect, then we usually try harder—try a different tactic, enlist another strategy or complete our Christian checklist. And when those attempts don't work, we may yield to temptation and take comfort where we can find it—in sinful escapes providing temporary pleasure.

Eventually, however, we realize we're facing a blind spot that requires an eternal perspective rather than an earthly one. As our spiritual eyes are washed clean of debris and adjust to looking at life through a divine lens, we realize God is working in us, through us and with us. His miracle is already being birthed from the mess we've made while looking for more.

- What item(s) do you lose or misplace most often? When was the last time the missing item was in plain sight in front of you?

- What would you like to experience in the present that you often assume can only happen in the future? What aspects of God's miracle for your life are you making conditional on the future?

Focus Your Vision

Sometimes in Scripture we find an encounter in which Jesus heals someone, and the scene ends there. We don't know what happened after Christ healed Peter's mother-in-law of her fever (Matthew 8:14–15) or restored the man with leprosy (Matthew 8:1–4) or raised the widow's son from the dead (Luke 7:11–17). In the case of the man blind from birth, however, the rest of the story—what happened after the man received his sight—is included.

Picking up with the consequences of the miracle the blind man received, notice how the various stakeholders regarded the gift he received. If you're part of a group study, invite someone to read the following passage aloud as everyone follows along. Then answer or discuss the questions that follow.

> After saying this, he [Jesus] spit on the ground, made some mud with the saliva, and put it on the man's eyes. "Go," he told him, "wash in the Pool of

Siloam" (this word means "Sent"). So the man went and washed, and came home seeing.

His neighbors and those who had formerly seen him begging asked, "Isn't this the same man who used to sit and beg?" Some claimed that he was.

Others said, "No, he only looks like him."

But he himself insisted, "I am the man."

"How then were your eyes opened?" they asked.

He replied, "The man they call Jesus made some mud and put it on my eyes. He told me to go to Siloam and wash. So I went and washed, and then I could see."

"Where is this man?" they asked him.

"I don't know," he said.

They brought to the Pharisees the man who had been blind. Now the day on which Jesus had made the mud and opened the man's eyes was a Sabbath. Therefore the Pharisees also asked him how he had received his sight. "He put mud on my eyes," the man replied, "and I washed, and now I see."

Some of the Pharisees said, "This man is not from God, for he does not keep the Sabbath."

But others asked, "How can a sinner perform such signs?" So they were divided.

Then they turned again to the blind man, "What have you to say about him? It was your eyes he opened."

The man replied, "He is a prophet."

John 9:6–17

- Why do you suppose many of the healed man's neighbors and acquaintances struggled to recognize him after his miracle? Other than being sighted, what else about the healed man might have changed?

- Why do those listening to the healed man's explanation of what happened to him still doubt his experience? How do you imagine he felt when they continued to doubt the miracle?

- Why does Jesus not fit the Pharisees' criteria for someone capable of miraculously healing this man's blindness? What tension exists because Jesus healed this man on the Jewish Sabbath, a traditional day of rest and religious reflection?

- Facing a dilemma about Jesus' identity and power, the Pharisees return to the healed man for his assessment. Why do you suppose he assumed Jesus was a prophet?

Seeing Is Believing

After the man blind since birth was healed, his neighbors tried to talk themselves out of the truth of the miracle standing before them. How could the blind beggar they had known for years suddenly be such a different person? Why was he now able to see? What miracle had occurred in their midst to bring about such results? Some acquaintances maintained it wasn't really the blind man they once knew—just someone who resembled him.

The people around this newly sighted, walking-and-talking miracle were so accustomed to viewing him one way, in one context, that they struggled to make the leap required to accept what had happened. They knew him as the blind man begging near the temple, and that was all he was to them, all he could ever be. This man had been forced to live with his limitations all his life, and those he encountered regularly couldn't see past those limitations. Logic and probability told them that such a dramatic, sudden occurrence was simply not possible.

Seeing those people around him for the first time, the miracle man insisted he was the same person they had once known as the blind beggar. To help them understand the unimaginable healing that had taken place, he recounted the interaction with Jesus in a direct, straightforward manner. Like someone explaining something to others that he himself does not fully understand, the man probably realized how implausible his explanation sounded. He was undoubtedly still processing that day's events himself.

Rarely if ever had a stranger shown up, spit on the ground, made mud, caked it over a blind man's eyes and then told him to go wash them in order to see. When the bystanders asked, "Where is this man who healed you?" the man told them, "I don't know." They might as well have asked him *who* was this man and *how* did he heal you—because the sighted man didn't know the answers to those questions either.

This miracle recipient told the truth of his messy miracle and its transforming power in his life, but he didn't really know any more about what had happened than those interrogating him did. Surely he must have felt a bit overwhelmed. Having been blind since birth, this man was now getting used to seeing colors, shapes, depth, light, faces, textures—everything! Apparently, the change in his life caused those who once knew him to doubt he could be the same man. And perhaps this made sense to him because he might have wondered the same thing along with them: *Who have I now become?*

Perhaps you have failed to recognize someone well-known to you because you weren't expecting to see them in a context different from your usual encounters. You may have had someone struggle to recognize you in like manner. It's easy to get so familiar with seeing people a certain way, in a certain place with certain limitations, that we miss seeing below the surface.

You may also fail to recognize yourself in the midst of your mess—and in the midst of God's miracle. When you're mired in the mud of life, you may struggle and long for more because you know you haven't experienced all that God has for you, all that He created you to be. And then when you experience His miracle, you may be stunned to come to terms with your new self. You knew who you used to be, but suddenly your life has changed. Then you're forced to see yourself not through your own eyes or anyone else's, but only as God sees you.

- How have you experienced uncertainty about who you are in the midst of your mess? In the midst of God's miracle for you?

- When have you not felt seen by those around you in the midst of a struggle, hardship or limitation? How did you handle their inability or unwillingness to recognize what you were going through?

- When have you seen someone else, overlooked by others, who needed your help or encouragement? How were you able to minister to them by meeting a need?

- What aspects of your messiness cause you to fear judgment, criticism or rejection from others? How do you usually handle situations in which you feel vulnerable because of the mess you're in?

Miracle in Your Mess

If you've ever watched a plant, animal or child grow and mature, then you know how an organism in transition can look radically different from day to day, week to week, month to month. What begins as a tiny green sprout barely breaking the soil becomes a stalk with leaves, then blossoms. The newborn puppy or kitten you can hold in your hands grows into the pet that's ten times their size at birth. Babies become toddlers who become children who go through preadolescence and then the teen years. All living things that grow develop through stages that change aspects of their appearance but not their essence.

Your spiritual development goes through a similar growth process as you begin seeing more clearly how God is at work in your life. When you

51

encounter the sight-giving, life-changing, heart-softening power of Jesus, you are no longer who you once were. You may feel a bit disoriented with yourself as you begin to realize the major shift occurring inside you.

Family, friends, loved ones and coworkers may notice a change in you, recognizing that you are no longer the same person they used to know. Because you are a follower of Jesus who walks in faith by the power of the Spirit, your attitude, speech and behavior change, sometimes dramatically. The thoughts and activities that used to captivate you no longer hold the same appeal when your focus shifts to knowing the Lord and serving Him. God's Word tells us, "Therefore, if anyone is in Christ, he is a new creation; old things have passed away; behold, all things have become new" (2 Corinthians 5:17 NKJV).

When you accept the free gift of salvation through the death and resurrection of Jesus Christ, you see things differently. Earthly appetites and personal defenses begin to dissolve as you're nourished by God's Word and fellowship with other believers. Old pursuits and addictive habits lose their power over you. You realize that some relationships that once sustained you were actually holding you back. Your eyes become focused on an eternal perspective that glorifies God and advances His Kingdom.

Sure, you might stumble or fall occasionally before getting back on your feet. But God will always be there to lift you, hold you, guide you and empower you to start walking again. The process is usually messy, requiring twists and turns, disappointments and surprises. Throughout your journey, however, you can trust that God is always working for your good no matter your circumstances, relational status, income bracket, education level, age or stage. Just because you cannot see His miracle starting to grow in the muddy soil of your mistakes does not mean there are no seeds taking root.

- When have you grown impatient with your spiritual progress because of ongoing struggles? What obstacles have been the most challenging to your growth?

- What are some signs, small and subtle or big and bold, you've noticed that God is already at work in your mess to produce His miracle?

- What are some ways you've changed since becoming a follower of Jesus? What areas of your life continue to cause conflict or distress because of your new identity in Christ?

- If you could ask God to immediately remove one obstacle or thorn in your flesh, something that you believe hinders your spiritual growth, what would it be? Why?

—————— LOOK AGAIN ——————

Refuse to let anything prevent you from seeing all that the Lord has for you. If it is not holy, you do not want it. If it is not blessed, you do not need it. If it is not going to give God all the glory, then you do not desire any part of it.

Your Mess, God's Miracle, chapter 3, page 68

Similar to the previous sessions, the questions and exercises below provide opportunities for further exploration of this material to help you put these truths into practice. If you're participating in a group study, use these as a personal way to stay connected to what you've been thinking and feeling since your last group session and to prepare for your group's next meeting. The more aware you become of the way God is working to bring His miracle to life in the midst of your messes, the stronger your faith becomes.

You will benefit from reading chapter 3 in *Your Mess, God's Miracle* before completing the questions and exercises that follow. Once again, answer and respond in the spaces provided below or use your own journal or notebook to collect all pieces of this study together in one place. Remember, this isn't homework and shouldn't feel like an obligation. Spend a few moments in prayer and ask the Holy Spirit to guide you as you reflect on, engage with and implement what's necessary for you to see clearly and experience more of God's power in the midst of your messy life.

See the Light

Doubt and despair are two of the enemy's greatest tools for blinding you to God's power and goodness. The devil knows that if he can wedge his lies into your thinking, then he can blind you to what God's doing in your life. And when you're unable to see yourself, your life and God clearly, then you're more prone to wander into darkness. When you can't see where you're going spiritually, then you're more likely to feel alone, isolated and separated from God and His people.

One of the best ways to dispel this tactic of the enemy is to stay grounded in the truth of God's Word. Especially as you begin allowing your heart to hope for more—more joy and peace, more purpose and passion—you will find that meditating and reflecting on passages of Scripture provides clarity, insight and illumination into those messy areas of life. While exploring the beauty and wisdom of the Psalms is always beneficial, some are particularly helpful as you transition into the miracle God has for you.

Such is the case with Psalm 107 below, which describes a variety of situations in which God meets His children right where they are—whether in a desert wasteland, a dark prison or a storm-tossed sea. As you read through this psalm, underline or circle the words, phrases and images that stand out to you. Think about how and where you need the Lord to meet you right now as you complete the questions that follow.

> Give thanks to the Lord, for he is good;
>   his love endures forever.
>
> Let the redeemed of the Lord tell their story—
>   those he redeemed from the hand of the foe,
> those he gathered from the lands,
>   from east and west, from north and south.
>
> Some wandered in desert wastelands,
>   finding no way to a city where they could settle.
> They were hungry and thirsty,
>   and their lives ebbed away.
> Then they cried out to the Lord in their trouble,
>   and he delivered them from their distress.
> He led them by a straight way
>   to a city where they could settle.
> Let them give thanks to the Lord for his unfailing love
>   and his wonderful deeds for mankind,
> for he satisfies the thirsty
>   and fills the hungry with good things.
>
> Some sat in darkness, in utter darkness,
>   prisoners suffering in iron chains,
> because they rebelled against God's commands
>   and despised the plans of the Most High.

So he subjected them to bitter labor;
　　they stumbled, and there was no one to help.
Then they cried to the LORD in their trouble,
　　and he saved them from their distress.
He brought them out of darkness, the utter darkness,
　　and broke away their chains.
Let them give thanks to the LORD for his unfailing love
　　and his wonderful deeds for mankind,
for he breaks down gates of bronze
　　and cuts through bars of iron.

Some became fools through their rebellious ways
　　and suffered affliction because of their iniquities.
They loathed all food
　　and drew near the gates of death.
Then they cried to the LORD in their trouble,
　　and he saved them from their distress.
He sent out his word and healed them;
　　he rescued them from the grave.
Let them give thanks to the LORD for his unfailing love
　　and his wonderful deeds for mankind.
Let them sacrifice thank offerings
　　and tell of his works with songs of joy.

Some went out on the sea in ships;
　　they were merchants on the mighty waters.
They saw the works of the LORD,
　　his wonderful deeds in the deep.
For he spoke and stirred up a tempest
　　that lifted high the waves.
They mounted up to the heavens and went down to the depths;
　　in their peril their courage melted away.
They reeled and staggered like drunkards;
　　they were at their wits' end.
Then they cried out to the LORD in their trouble,
　　and he brought them out of their distress.
He stilled the storm to a whisper;
　　the waves of the sea were hushed.

They were glad when it grew calm,
    and he guided them to their desired haven.
Let them give thanks to the LORD for his unfailing love
    and his wonderful deeds for mankind.
Let them exalt him in the assembly of the people
    and praise him in the council of the elders.

He turned rivers into a desert,
    flowing springs into thirsty ground,
and fruitful land into a salt waste,
    because of the wickedness of those who lived there.
He turned the desert into pools of water
    and the parched ground into flowing springs;
there he brought the hungry to live,
    and they founded a city where they could settle.
They sowed fields and planted vineyards
    that yielded a fruitful harvest;
he blessed them, and their numbers greatly increased,
    and he did not let their herds diminish.

Then their numbers decreased, and they were humbled
    by oppression, calamity and sorrow;
he who pours contempt on nobles
    made them wander in a trackless waste.
But he lifted the needy out of their affliction
    and increased their families like flocks.
The upright see and rejoice,
    but all the wicked shut their mouths.

Let the one who is wise heed these things
    and ponder the loving deeds of the LORD.

Psalm 107

- Look back at the words you underlined or circled in this psalm. Do you see a pattern or common theme? What might God be telling you through this psalm right now?

- What are some of God's miraculous deeds described or summarized throughout this psalm? How does He meet people with exactly what they need in each situation?

- Looking back on your life and times when God has protected you, provided for you and promoted you in the past, what have you learned about yourself? About God's ability to meet you where you are?

- What does it mean for you to "heed these things and ponder the loving deeds of the LORD" (verse 43), considering where you are right now in your life? How can praising and thanking God prepare your heart for the miracle God is birthing in your mess?

Fresh Perspective

God is always at work in your life, whether you see it—or see it the way you expect to see it—or not. But the more clearly you can see, the more you can prepare, accept and exercise faith in the One who loves you better than anyone else does. In his letter to the believers in the early Church at Ephesus, Paul wrote, "I pray that the eyes of your heart may be enlightened in order that you may know the hope to which he has called you, the riches of his glorious inheritance in his holy people, and his incomparably great power for us who believe" (Ephesians 1:18–19).

Learning to open your eyes and see beyond what your human eyes register occurs as you mature in your faith and experience more of God's presence and power: "For we walk by faith, not by sight" (2 Corinthians 5:7 ESV). As the eyes of your heart grow accustomed to seeing beyond what is merely visible in the earthly realms, you realize so much more is going on.

You recognize what you're missing when you stray from God and rely on your own power to try to change. You see through the devil's schemes and snares that obscure your vision to the truth. And you gaze into the eyes of Jesus, following His example as you become willing to suffer the temporary growing pains of this life so that you can produce the mature, spiritual fruit God designed you to experience.

Seeing clearly is essential if you are to grow in your faith and persevere through the mud and muck of life's messes. When you place your hope in the Lord, you see beyond the circumstances, events and emotions trying to blind you. God's Word makes this contrast between what you see with your physical eyes and what you see with the eyes of your heart even sharper: "As we look not to the things that are seen but to the things that are unseen. For the things that are seen are transient, but the things that are unseen are eternal" (2 Corinthians 4:18 ESV).

- How often are you aware of seeing beyond what is visible with your eyes? How attuned are the eyes of your heart to the spiritual realities taking place in your life?

- What does developing an eternal perspective mean to you? How does focusing on the way God sees you and your life give you a bigger, broader sense of what's going on?

- How does being able to spot the snares and temptations of the enemy help you avoid them? How do you usually protect yourself when you realize you're being tempted and attacked spiritually?

- Based on what you see with the eyes of your heart right now, what do you want to tell God? What do you want to ask of Him? Spend some minutes in prayer, unplugged and undistracted, to open your heart and still yourself before the Lord. Make sure you spend some of this time listening for the voice of the Holy Spirit and the encouragement and instruction He may be speaking to you.

Watch Where You're Going

When you were growing up, at some point you probably planted seeds in a cup and watched new life take root and grow. It might have been for a school assignment, your own curiosity or an activity shared within your family. Even if you can't recall creating this kind of mini-garden as a kid, perhaps you have helped a child in your life plant seeds and watched them sprout, grow and bloom.

As you'll recall, dramatic changes often happen day to day and certainly week to week with such seedlings. And just because you cannot see what's going on beneath the soil doesn't mean nothing is happening. Growth takes place below the surface slowly and gradually before it bursts through the dirt to become visible. From there, depending on the kind of seed, visible growth may happen in leaps and bounds or continue being slow and steady. Regardless, the growth grounds you with tangible reminders that maturity and new life are a process.

Whether you consider yourself to have a green thumb or not, and no matter what time of the year it may be, it's time to plant a mini-miracle in a mud cup. You can likely complete this exercise with what you have on hand. Choose a hearty, fast-growing plant, flower or herb if possible—basil, mint and oregano work well, and so do marigolds, sunflowers and poppies. If you prefer veggies, then carrots, beets or peas might be best. It doesn't matter what you choose, so go with what's available, accessible and inexpensive.

Once you've selected your seed type, select a container. You can use a plastic or paper cup, an old coffee mug, a small jar or a leftover flowerpot. While you can use premixed potting soil if you wish, consider going outside and finding a spot where you can fill your container with dirt from the ground. You don't need to spit in it to make mud, but after your seed is planted, you will want to add a little water and place the container in a spot that gets enough light.

Before you dismiss this little gardening experiment as childish or predictable, allow for the possibility of learning something new about your own growth process. Focus on what's required for your seedling to grow—air, nutrients from the soil, water, light—and what's required for something new to take root in the messy soil of your life right now. Consider the necessity of patience and the joy that comes from witnessing small changes signaling greater growth.

Seeing God's Spirit in Action

Sometimes the process is messy. Sometimes the process is complicated. Sometimes we get dirty from living life before we get clean from the Giver of eternal life.

Your Mess, God's Miracle, chapter 4, page 75

May the God of hope fill you with all joy and peace as you trust in him, so that you may overflow with hope by the power of the Holy Spirit.

Romans 15:13

Open Your Eyes

You may not consider spit to be a supernatural conduit of healing power. But when the One spitting is the Son of God, suddenly saliva is not just a biological by-product for moistening one's mouth. In one of Jesus' messiest miracles, His spit becomes the glue between heaven and earth, between the holy and the broken, between the sighted and the blind.

The way Christ chose to heal the man blind since birth likely surprised everyone around Him—from the blind man to Jesus' disciples to bystanders and onlookers and eventually the Pharisees and religious leaders. Jesus did not simply lay hands on the blind man or pray over him; the Messiah connected the essence of His identity, the DNA contained in His spittle, with the portals of this man's need.

Jesus didn't simply choose to heal this man—He chose to heal him in a way that literally gave the blind man part of Himself so that the man might receive something he had lacked since birth: "Then he spit on the ground, made mud with the saliva, and spread the mud over the blind man's eyes" (John 9:6 NLT). Out of all the methods the Master could have chosen for imparting healing to this man blind from birth, Jesus chose the one that combined part of His divine humanity with the basest element available—dirt. The mud He mixed reflected the duality of Christ's identity as both God and man, part of the Creator and part of the creation.

Swirling His own spittle with dirt to make mud probably did not elevate the opinion of those watching what Jesus was doing. And then when He took a gob of the gooey brown stuff and gently spread it over the blind man's eyes, can't you just imagine what everyone must have thought? Who in the world spits, mixes mud from it and spreads the result over someone's eyes? Such actions created an unexpected scene that forced everyone around to pay attention. This Jesus of Nazareth, the One who said He was the Messiah, not only healed a blind man, but He did so in the most startling way.

Spitting, regardless of the time period or culture, has never been a particularly noble or dignified action. Most likely, expelling saliva from one's mouth was considered crude and impolite in public settings, much as we consider it today. The exception might be small children who simply don't know better or haven't yet been taught social etiquette. But there's Jesus spitting without hesitation and then kneeling down to mix His own saliva in the dusty ground until He'd formed a muddy paste.

Spit and mud are both very base, earthy, crude elements. Most, if not all, people at that time would never imagine placing mud made from their own spit onto the face of someone else. Wouldn't such an act seem irrational, childish and offensive?

Again, if it had been anyone else doing such an act, the answer would be yes. But when the Son of God performed such an act, the results produced a miracle. Fortunately for us today, we don't need our Savior's spit to access His healing, holy anointing and supernatural power. We don't need Christ's spit because we have His Spirit!

- What comes to mind when you think about spit or spitting? What did you learn growing up about when it's acceptable for you to spit?

- Why do you suppose Jesus chose such a surprising, earthy method for healing the blind man? What does the method Jesus used communicate about His identity and accessibility to us?

Focus Your Vision

Perhaps one of the reasons Jesus chose such a personal, unique method for healing the blind man emerges in the tension surrounding His identity as the Messiah. While speculation about Jesus' assertion to be the Son of God probably consumed public gossip throughout His public ministry, Jesus knew that healing the blind man—and on a Sabbath, no less—would attract the attention of the religious leaders and Pharisees already planning how to contain or eliminate Him.

And indeed it did! Even after the newly healed man testified before the Pharisees, they still refused to believe his story—largely because believing his account would force them to acknowledge the power of God demonstrated by Jesus. So instead, these Jewish religious leaders debated possibilities among themselves and decided to take their investigation even further. What if this man had only pretended to be blind and was now lying about the impact of what Jesus had done? As absurd and implausible as this sounds, these leaders sent for the healed man's parents, looking for leverage.

As you pick up the story at this point, consider what it must have been like for this man, blind since birth, who had been gifted with sight and yet was still doubted and harassed by those in power. Once again, if you're part of a group study, invite someone to read the following passage aloud as everyone follows along. Then answer or discuss the questions that follow.

> They [the Pharisees] still did not believe that he had been blind and had received his sight until they sent for the man's parents. "Is this your son?" they asked. "Is this the one you say was born blind? How is it that now he can see?"
>
> "We know he is our son," the parents answered, "and we know he was born blind. But how he can see now, or who opened his eyes, we don't know. Ask him. He is of age; he will speak for himself." His parents said this because they were afraid of the Jewish leaders, who already had decided that anyone who acknowledged that Jesus was the Messiah would be put out of the synagogue. That was why his parents said, "He is of age; ask him."
>
> A second time they summoned the man who had been blind. "Give glory to God by telling the truth," they said. "We know this man is a sinner."
>
> He replied, "Whether he is a sinner or not, I don't know. One thing I do know. I was blind but now I see!"
>
> Then they asked him, "What did he do to you? How did he open your eyes?"
>
> He answered, "I have told you already and you did not listen. Why do you want to hear it again? Do you want to become his disciples too?"
>
> Then they hurled insults at him and said, "You are this fellow's disciple! We are disciples of Moses! We know that God spoke to Moses, but as for this fellow, we don't even know where he comes from."
>
> The man answered, "Now that is remarkable! You don't know where he comes from, yet he opened my eyes. We know that God does not listen to sinners. He listens to the godly person who does his will. Nobody has ever heard of opening the eyes of a man born blind. If this man were not from God, he could do nothing."
>
> To this they replied, "You were steeped in sin at birth; how dare you lecture us!" And they threw him out.
>
> John 9:18–34

- Why did the parents of the man who had been blind answer the way they did when summoned before the Jewish religious leaders? What were they afraid would happen?

- What do you imagine the man gifted with sight must have been thinking and feeling when the Pharisees brought him before them a second time? Why?

- What signs do you see in the healed man's responses that reveal his frustration with the Pharisees' interrogation? How do the man's responses reveal his own uncertainty about the identity of Jesus?

- What's the logic behind the healed man's conclusion, "If this man were not from God, he could do nothing" (verse 33)? And how did the Pharisees respond in order to evade the truth and logic of what the healed man had inferred?

Seeing Is Believing

When Jesus healed the blind man, He was probably already getting a reputation. For someone saying He was the Son of God, the long-promised Messiah sent from the living God, holy and almighty, Jesus upended most people's expectations. Rather than being born in a royal palace or to a prestigious family of devout Jews, He was born in a dirty, smelly cowshed in the middle of nowhere—the little sheep town of Bethlehem. Instead of having parents who were educated, wealthy or religious leaders, Jesus was born of a young virgin engaged to a carpenter from Nazareth.

In addition to such humble, unremarkable beginnings, Jesus didn't seek out the politicians, temple leaders or Jewish zealots. Instead, He deliberately mingled with known sinners—some of whom became His devoted followers, such as Matthew, who had been a tax collector, one of the most despised professions in Israel (Matthew 9:9–13). Jesus talked to a prostitute and accepted her intimate gift of washing His feet with her tears (Luke 7:38–44). He also refused to condemn a woman caught in adultery who was brought before Him and instead turned the tables on her accusers (John 8:1–11). Christ interacted with lepers and soldiers, widows and children, fishermen and Samaritan women. Clearly, He didn't mind getting dirty or worry about what others, especially the religious elite, thought of Him.

So nothing about the way the Pharisees interrogated the man He had just healed surprised Jesus. Because they refused to accept the truth of His identity, they had to find ways to deny, ignore and detach from the reality of His divinity. Even before these Jewish leaders started fretting about this miracle, Jesus confronted the misconception held by His own disciples, who had asked, "Rabbi, who sinned, this man or his parents, that he was born blind?" (John 9:2).

Their question was most likely an honest one, not a mean-spirited or disparaging one. According to Jewish Law, most sins were manifest by their consequences and external appearances rather than internal motives and heart attitudes. By focusing primarily on outward acts and appearances, the religious leaders of that time became legalists, concerned more with fulfilling the Law than with relating to the God who had given them the Law. As long as they maintained a pious, self-righteous public persona, they didn't look at their impure thoughts, evil intentions and blatant hypocrisy.

Such legalism provided no justification for their sinful ways. Even before Christ's time on earth, God has always focused on relating to His children as a loving Father, not a vengeful judge. God has always been concerned foremost with what's in our hearts. When He was instructing the prophet Samuel to anoint the next king of Israel, David, God stated, "For the LORD sees not as man sees: man looks on the outward appearance, but the LORD looks on the heart" (1 Samuel 16:7 ESV). David was the youngest in his family, and even his own father overlooked him when Samuel came knocking in search of the next king. But God chose David because he was a man after God's own heart, not because he looked like what others expected a king to look like.

This interior spiritual focus also explains why Jesus repeatedly rebuked the Pharisees and Sadducees for their hypocrisy. The double standard of their hypocrisy is aptly illustrated by the problem with a dirty dish: "Woe to you, teachers of the law and Pharisees, you hypocrites! You clean the outside of the cup and dish, but inside they are full of greed and self-indulgence. Blind Pharisee! First clean the inside of the cup and dish, and then the outside also will be clean" (Matthew 23:25–26).

Jesus made it clear that we must begin from the inside out, with our hearts. And Jesus is the only way we can cleanse our hearts and follow through with our obedience. Which brings us back to His answer to the disciples' question about a causal correlation between sin and the blind man's condition: "Neither this man nor his parents sinned . . . but this happened so that the works of God might be displayed in him" (John 9:3).

The works of God continue to be displayed in your life as well.

He sees your heart and meets you in the messy mud with more than just spit.

You have the gift of the Holy Spirit not only to heal you, but also to sustain you.

- When have your expectations about who God is and what He can do been turned inside out? What did you discover about Him that you didn't already know?

- How have you struggled with legalism—a focus on obedience for its own sake rather than to love and serve God—in your life? What prevents you from drifting into legalism now?

- Where do you see the works of God on display in your life? What has He helped you overcome that you could never have conquered on your own?

- If Jesus saw you in your messiest, most painful, most broken moments, what would He see? What do you believe He would say to you?

Miracle in Your Mess

The way Jesus chose to heal the man blind since birth highlights the way Jesus continues to restore your sight today. Just as He spit, muddied His fingers and smeared the moist earth over the blind man's eyes, Christ shares who He is, God's only Son, with you in the places where you feel the most shame, the most pain and the most distress. Jesus is always willing to enter into your messiness, your murkiness, your muddiness and your most unmanageable mistakes. Some of your muddiness may be residual from before you met Christ. Some of your dirt may be from the ongoing struggle to experience the fullness of your new identity in Him.

Even after you come to know the Lord and experience the indwelling of the Holy Spirit, you may find yourself playing in the mud from time to time, slipping back into old habits and negative thought patterns, leaving room for the enemy to tempt you further and pull you away from God. It might be wrestling with an ongoing dependence on alcohol or prescription painkillers. Perhaps you're always comparing yourself to others and trying to outdo them with how you present yourself on social media. It could be surfing online for images that ignite lust in your heart. You might be making money your idol in the way you view, save or spend it. Nearly everyone battles scuff marks and dirt stains that can come from living in our world today.

But you mustn't lose heart or give up hope. You must fight the good fight and rely on the power of God's Spirit in you to strengthen you in your weakness and to sustain you in your walk with God. Paul described the tension of our divinely muddy lives when he wrote, "For I know that good itself does not dwell in me, that is, in my sinful nature. For I have the desire to do what is good, but I cannot carry it out. For I do not do the good I want to do, but the evil I do not want to do—this I keep on doing" (Romans 7:18–19).

When Jesus used His holy spit, which contained His divine DNA, to make mud for a miracle, He also reached into the messy, dirty struggles of your life. By instructing the blind man to go and wash in the Pool of Siloam, Christ reminds you to focus on the perfect outcome as well as the messy method. Sometimes you may feel so bogged down in your temporary mess that you lose sight of the permanence of God's promises.

While the God of the outcome is the same God of the process, you may feel so blinded by your pain, disappointment, anger and grief that you become disoriented about what's true. You may start to confuse what you're going through with where you're going to. But persevering in all the hard challenges is only worth it if you realize what God has prepared for you, not just in heaven but here on earth.

Life on our planet right now often feels brutal and overwhelming. The world seems to have spun off its axis, leaving collateral damage from pandemics, politics and pandemonium left and right. Expenses soar while income falters. Relationships crumble while hearts grow harder. Families become fragmented, and communities seem irreparably divided. You may be fighting depression, anxiety, fear, anger and doubt on a daily, or even hourly, basis.

But no matter what you're going through, you must remember this: Your temporary has run its course while your permanent is just getting started. Because if you're going through what you've never experienced before, then it's only because you're about to step into what you've never stepped into before!

- What sinful struggles and temptations presently hinder your spiritual growth? How are you surrendering them to the power of Christ in you?

- When have you most recently experienced the tension between doing what your old, sinful self craves and doing what your new, redeemed self knows God wants you to do?

- What are some ways you sometimes become too focused on the temporary, muddy methods rather than the eternal, holy outcomes?

- Choose a favorite verse or passage from God's Word that reminds you to look beyond your present struggles to see your glorious future. Use this verse or passage as a springboard for spending a few minutes in prayer, thanking God for all He's already doing and anticipating all that He's about to do.

LOOK AGAIN

> Too often . . . we want dates, times and details from God when He wants to give us more of His Spirit and more of His power. We are focused on the "when," and He is focused on giving us the "how."
>
> *Your Mess, God's Miracle*, chapter 4, page 84

Once again, use the following questions and prompts to enhance your ability to see all that God is doing in your life right now. Remember that as your spiritual vision becomes sharper, clearer and more acute, you will likely notice details and subtleties you might have overlooked before. These could include thought patterns and attitudes as well as habits you know are blocking your spiritual growth. You may notice greater temptations coming your way, a sure sign the enemy doesn't like your progress and spiritual growth.

You might also glimpse indications of the miracle God is working from your mess. These could be internal, subtle shifts or external, overt changes. Whatever you're noticing, listen for the voice of the Holy Spirit; He may be speaking into your life right now. As usual, jot down your answers in the space provided or continue using the journal or notebook you've started. If you're part of a group completing this study, use this "Look Again" section as a personal time of exploring and engaging with everything you're learning.

See the Light

Jesus gifted the blind man with spit-infused mud that resulted in sight for the first time in his life. Jesus has gifted you with Spirit-infused power to see clearly and to experience His miracle in the midst of life's messes. Even though you're aware of this divine gift and have experienced times of power, peace and purpose, you may still struggle to receive the fullness of the Spirit and His gifts.

Most likely, you tend to think of gifts as more tangible tokens of someone's love for you or practical tools given to improve your life. Perhaps Christmas or birthday presents come to mind, large items that surprised and delighted you when you unwrapped the festive paper covering their contents. The very best gifts, however, usually exceed your expectations. These are the gifts for which you barely recognized a need, but for which someone else could see your need better than you could. Such is the case with the gift Jesus left His followers, to which He had alluded even before His death and resurrection:

> If you love me, keep my commands. And I will ask the Father, and he will give you another advocate to help you and be with you forever—the Spirit of truth. The world cannot accept him, because it neither sees him nor knows him. But you know him, for he lives with you and will be in you. I will not leave you as orphans; I will come to you. Before long, the world will not see me anymore, but you will see me. Because I live, you also will live. On that day you will realize that I am in my Father, and you are in me, and I am in you. Whoever has my commands and keeps them is the one who loves me. The one who loves me will be loved by my Father, and I too will love them and show myself to them.
>
> John 14:15–21

After rising from the dead, but before He ascended into heaven, Jesus knew the time was approaching, and He wanted to make sure His disciples knew the gift He had promised was about to be unwrapped:

> After his suffering, he presented himself to them and gave many convincing proofs that he was alive. He appeared to them over a period of forty days and spoke about the kingdom of God. On one occasion, while he was eating with them, he gave them this command: "Do not leave Jerusalem, but wait for the gift my Father promised, which you have heard me speak about. For John baptized with water, but in a few days you will be baptized with the Holy Spirit."
>
> Then they gathered around him and asked him, "Lord, are you at this time going to restore the kingdom to Israel?"
>
> He said to them: "It is not for you to know the times or dates the Father has set by his own authority. But you will receive power when the Holy Spirit comes on you; and you will be my witnesses in Jerusalem, and in all Judea and Samaria, and to the ends of the earth."
>
> After he said this, he was taken up before their very eyes, and a cloud hid him from their sight.

They were looking intently up into the sky as he was going, when suddenly two men dressed in white stood beside them. "Men of Galilee," they said, "why do you stand here looking into the sky? This same Jesus, who has been taken from you into heaven, will come back in the same way you have seen him go into heaven."

Acts 1:3–11

Even if He hadn't been omniscient, Jesus knew the disciples well enough to realize they were making plans for when He would no longer be with them. Which is why He commanded them to sit tight until they received the gift of the Holy Spirit. And how did they respond to their Master's instruction? They gathered around Jesus and asked if this would be when He restored the kingdom of Israel. Basically, they wanted to know dates and details of when Christ would overthrow the Romans and reestablish Israel's independence. Because surely that was His purpose as the Messiah, right?

Their response reveals the same expectation we often fall into still today. We want to access God's power and harness it for the purposes that seem sensible and logical to us, rather than using that power to experience the miracle God wants to give us. Jesus' followers during His time on earth felt the same way. Even after all they had been through together, after all they had heard Jesus say and the miracles they had witnessed Him perform, they assumed Jesus was going to restore Israel through earthly methods. Jesus, however, made it clear that their attention was misfocused: "It is not for you to know the times or dates the Father has set by his own authority" (Acts 1:7). Instead, He wanted them to focus on the power they would receive through the Holy Spirit, which would allow them to share the Gospel throughout the known world and to the ends of the earth.

Maybe you're waiting on dates, times and details from God before you move forward into your miracle. Perhaps you're focused on the "when" and He's focused on giving you the "how" right now. Because you cannot see a way forward out of your mess, you may be waiting for the Lord to spell it out for you. But you know what? The Lord may be waiting on you to receive what He's already given you!

Getting hung up about the details of what God's doing in your life may cause you to miss out on the delivery. When you're focused only on how messy your process seems, you may miss out on the miracle of His promise.

When you're blinded by the temporary obstacles of the present, you might miss out on the eternal perspective of your future.

When you think you need to understand how the miracle works before you receive it, then you're likely getting in the way of what God wants to give you. Sometimes your logical, analytical human brain impedes your ability to receive the power of God's Spirit in your life. Sometimes old attitudes and assumptions must be dispelled before you can fully embrace the truth of God's purpose for your life. Sometimes your time to receive is right now!

- Do you think of yourself as more of a detail-oriented person or a big picture–oriented person? Does the same tendency hold true in your spiritual life?

- Describe a time when you were waiting on God to reveal, instruct or answer, only to realize He was waiting on you. What did you take away from this experience?

- How would you describe your relationship with the Holy Spirit? Throughout any given day, how aware are you of walking in the Spirit to accomplish what's set before you?

- What do you sense God wants to do right now in your life? What miracle is He bringing to fruition sooner than you expected?

Fresh Perspective

When the followers of Jesus received the gift of the Holy Spirit, it was unmistakable. No matter how focused on details and misconceptions they might have been prior to His arrival, the dramatic entrance of God's Spirit made quite an impact:

> When the day of Pentecost came, they were all together in one place. Suddenly a sound like the blowing of a violent wind came from heaven and filled the whole house where they were sitting. They saw what seemed to be tongues of fire that separated and came to rest on each of them. All of them were filled with the Holy Spirit and began to speak in other tongues as the Spirit enabled them.
>
> Acts 2:1–4

Speaking in spiritual tongues, the followers of Jesus began to attract a crowd of various people because of the number of diverse languages they were speaking. Apparently, these onlookers assumed these newly Spirit-filled believers to be drunk on wine, but then Peter seized the opportunity to preach the Gospel. Immediately, the power and movement of this new Spirit speaking through Peter made an enormous impact for God's Kingdom: "Those who accepted his message were baptized, and about three thousand were added to their number that day" (Acts 2:41). And this was just the beginning! Throughout the New Testament, there are numerous examples of how the Holy Spirit continued to work in believers' lives in the early Church.

Without a doubt, the power those followers of Jesus received is the same power you received when you accepted God's gift of salvation through Jesus Christ and invited the Spirit to dwell in your heart. If you haven't accepted this free gift and invited God's Spirit into your heart, then now is the perfect time. The Bible promises, "The Spirit of God, who raised Jesus from the dead, lives in you. And just as God raised Christ Jesus from the dead, he will give life to your mortal bodies by this same Spirit living within you" (Romans 8:11 NLT).

No matter how messy your life is, you have the resurrection power of Jesus Christ dwelling in you. The same kind of death-conquering power that resurrected Jesus from the grave! With the power of the Holy Spirit in you, nothing is impossible. Your marriage can be resurrected. Your finances can rebound. Your losses can be restored. Your wounds can be healed. Your addictions can be eradicated. No matter what mess is trying to pull you down, you have the power—through the Holy Spirit—to overcome it! You have miracle-making power inside you.

Simply allow the mud to fall away so that you can see clearly. Stop assuming your miracle will happen at some future date. You only have to step out in faith and discover all that God has for you. Stop looking for what you can't see and focus in on what God has placed before you. Don't look down; look up!

No matter how dirty, muddy or grimy your situation appears, once you've welcomed the resurrection power of God's Spirit into your life, then you can see clearly how to move forward. No matter how often you've messed up, given in, fallen down or failed to see what God's doing in your life, you have the ability to remove all blinders and walk in the light!

- How has the Holy Spirit helped you see clearly as you move beyond your mess and step into God's miracle? How has the Spirit guided and directed you?

- How does knowing you have the resurrection power of Jesus inside you change your perspective on the messy parts of your life?

- What's the next step of faith, no matter how small or how big, you sense God wants you to take? What's been holding you back more— internal obstacles or external obstacles?

- How has your perception of your life's messiness changed since you began this study? Why has it changed?

Watch Where You're Going

There's no better way to get more acquainted with the Holy Spirit than to spend some time alone in prayer. You don't need to use formal language or pray out loud. You don't need to worry about finding the "right way" because any time you still yourself before God and open your heart to Him, communication takes place. Making prayer a consistent part of each day, throughout your day, will draw you closer to God's heart and help you experience the miracle He's unveiling in your midst.

Perhaps you already prioritize prayer as part of your day, and if that's the case, then you may want to find a fresh approach by changing the setting, the time or the way you usually pray. But the simplest way is to remove all or as many distractions and potential interruptions as possible and find a quiet place where you can converse with God. While you might be tempted to assume that God prefers quality communication over the quantity of your communication, the Bible makes it clear that He wants both.

God wants both your full attention and your heart engaged throughout everything you're doing throughout every day. If you're only praying because you know you're supposed to pray, then you're missing out on knowing God at a deeper level and experiencing the unlimited power of His Spirit. And if you're only praying when you're in need, in crisis or desperate for help beyond your own abilities, then that's not cultivating a relationship. That's viewing God as your supernatural problem solver.

If you look at the example of Jesus, during His time on earth He maintained both the quality of deep connection with His heavenly Father as well as consistency. Often Christ would slip away from the noise and bustle of those around Him and retreat to a quiet place so He could talk to God. Mark's gospel tells us, "Very early in the morning, while it was still dark, Jesus got up, left the house and went off to a solitary place, where he prayed" (Mark 1:35). This was not an isolated incident; throughout the gospel accounts of Jesus' life, you'll find more than three dozen occasions when Jesus prayed.

Prayer has been said to be the lifeblood of the Christian faith. And if you think about how vital healthy blood flow is for your body to function, then prayer plays a similar essential, life-giving role. Prayer is simply communicating with God and listening to what He wants to tell you. So look at your schedule and choose an hour this week when you can break with your normal routines and commitments and head to a quiet place where you won't be interrupted.

Begin your time by asking the Holy Spirit to move in you and through you as you seek to know more of God and open your heart to Him. Then spend a few minutes praising and worshiping God, giving thanks for the blessings in your life. From there, let God know where you are spiritually and what you think you need. Ask Him to provide what He knows you need even if that varies from the way you see things. Finally, spend at least five minutes in silence intently listening to the whisper of God's Spirit. After you have completed your prayer date with the Holy Spirit, answer the following questions.

- As you recall the time you spent in prayer, what stands out to you? How did you experience your time with God?

- On a scale of 1 to 10, with 1 being "rarely" and 10 being "constantly," how often would you say you pray most days? How could you incorporate more prayer moments into your day?

- How can dedicated time in prayer help you see your mess and God's miracle more clearly? What other benefits have you experienced from praying with full engagement on a regular basis?

- What did you hear when listening silently for the Spirit to speak? What next step does He want you to take?

Seeing What You've Never Seen Before

So how do we cultivate good soil in our lives so that we grow in the Spirit and produce good fruit? By infusing our dirt with the divine! Just as Jesus spit to make mud for the blind man's miracle, we must live in the fullness of the Holy Spirit and pour His power into the ground of our lives.

Your Mess, God's Miracle, chapter 5, page 102

"What no eye has seen,
  what no ear has heard,
and what no human mind has conceived"—
  the things God has prepared for those who love him.

1 Corinthians 2:9

Open Your Eyes

Sometimes life unfolds in the ways we hope and expect. Our physical bodies enjoy health and vibrancy, free of disease, injury or impairment. Our families remain stable and loving. Our jobs utilize and our co-workers value our contributions and hard work. Our communities thrive with support, service and sacrifice for one another. Our churches provide fellowship and meet the needs both within and outside the body of Christ.

During these moments and seasons, we believe we see God at work in ways that align with our understanding of who He is and what He's all about. We worship all facets of who He is—Father, Son and Holy Spirit—and we praise Him for the many blessings in our lives. We feel empowered and equipped to live out our God-given, anointed purpose in life and receive affirmation and validation from those around us. We sense our faith growing stronger, our spiritual vision becoming clearer and our relationship with the Lord developing the intimacy with Him we've longed to experience.

If these descriptions accurately reflect your life right now, then your blessings are overflowingly abundant. If these descriptions sound idealistic and unrealistic, however, then your blessings are also overflowingly abundant. Just because you're not experiencing life in the ways you want when you want it does not mean that God is not present, powerful and passionately in pursuit of your heart.

When you're blinded by the messy mud in your eyes, it's often challenging to see a bigger picture, a clearer perspective and an eternal glimpse of your life. When you begin to see what you've never seen before, it can feel disorienting and unsettling, challenging the story you've been telling yourself about who you are, what your life looks like and who God is. This narrative you tell yourself has largely developed based on your life experiences.

Beginning at birth, nearly all human beings develop coping methods and strategies for interacting with the people and environment around them. As we experience pain, disappointment and anger over unmet healthy needs, we often make inaccurate assumptions and false conclusions about who we are and what our place in the world will be. Our human nature, mostly relying on the ways our brains process and assess our experiences, leaves us with an incomplete view of ourselves and our lives.

As we grow and mature into adolescence and adulthood, more layers are added to our way of seeing ourselves and the world around us. Others' opinions and offenses, traumatic experiences and events and our subjective interpretation of all the incoming data may collide into a life saturated with heartache, loneliness and despair. The truth of who God says we are, how He loves us and has a purpose for us and how He wants us to live in relationship with Him gets distorted as well.

If you continue telling yourself the same old story and living the outdated scripts of your past, then it's hard to get the mud out of the way to see and experience the new story God has for you. Accepting the power of Christ through the indwelling of the Holy Spirit means realizing there's a new story, one that includes seeing what you've never seen before.

- If your life was made into a novel or movie, what would be the main plot elements or genre? What's the basis for your answer?

- What have you never seen before—about yourself, your life, your relationship with God—that you long to see clearly now? What's required to cleanse your vision from the muddy mess of life?

Focus Your Vision

The blind man Jesus healed probably held certain false beliefs about himself and his story. There was no way for him to learn to read or get an education because the Braille writing system had not been invented yet. Consequently, those around him—even his parents and family—might have assumed he

86

wasn't intelligent, capable or talented. Without the training to work in the skilled trades of that time, the blind man assumed his only option was to beg, hoping others would take pity on him and help him survive from day to day. Without any supporting resources, this blind man might have assumed his impairment was his identity. He was a blind beggar, and that's all he would ever be.

However, when this man washed away the miraculous mud mixed by Jesus, everything about the way he saw himself changed in an instant. Perhaps he immediately glimpsed his reflection on the surface of the water, experiencing light, shapes, colors and textures for the first time in his entire life. Everything he saw was new and startling because he had never seen any of it—or anything—prior to this life-changing event.

This man's new story didn't end there, however. Remember how the locals who knew this man only as the blind beggar doubted it was the same sighted man standing before them (John 9:8–9)? In addition to the open, penetrating gaze with which he saw them, something about this man's countenance must have looked different. He was no longer who he had once thought he was, so therefore they were confused as well.

Even after the man assured them he was, indeed, the person who had been blind since birth, they remained curious and somewhat skeptical. How in the world could he suddenly see? They wanted to know how the man had regained his sight, and then when he told them, they wanted to know where this healer was. And when he could not tell them, they brought him to the Pharisees. Suddenly, this man's messy miracle became even messier as he realized he was in the crosshairs of his healer's enemies.

The Jewish religious leaders then interrogated the newly miracle-made man not just once, but *twice*, and even called in his parents to testify. Then when the man pushed back and challenged the perceptions the Pharisees held, they insulted him and had him thrown out. But his story wasn't over—because that's when the impact of Jesus in his life was confirmed:

> Jesus heard that they had thrown him out, and when he found him, he said, "Do you believe in the Son of Man?"
>
> "Who is he, sir?" the man asked. "Tell me so that I may believe in him."
>
> Jesus said, "You have now seen him; in fact, he is the one speaking with you."
>
> Then the man said, "Lord, I believe," and he worshiped him.

Jesus said, "For judgment I have come into this world, so that the blind will see and those who see will become blind."

Some Pharisees who were with him heard him say this and asked, "What? Are we blind too?"

Jesus said, "If you were blind, you would not be guilty of sin; but now that you claim you can see, your guilt remains."

John 9:35–41

- When have you been forced to readjust the way you saw yourself and your life after an unexpected event? What changed in how you saw things?

- How does experiencing God's miraculous power in your mess require you to change the inaccurate story you've been telling yourself?

- Why do you suppose Jesus went and found the man He had healed after the Pharisees threw him out? What unfinished business did the two of them have?

- How does Jesus change the meaning of blindness from a physical condition to a spiritual one as He concludes their conversation?

Seeing Is Believing

When you accept the free gift of salvation through Jesus Christ and welcome the indwelling of His Spirit into your heart, you experience what Jesus called being "born again" (John 3:3). Just as your body arrived in this world at your birth, when you accept and receive Christ, "the Spirit gives birth to spirit" (John 3:6).

This spiritual birth means you are no longer the person you used to be. Being born again means you're about to see things you've never seen before. "This means that anyone who belongs to Christ has become a new person. The old life is gone; a new life has begun!" (2 Corinthians 5:17 NLT). Your new life comes from your relationship with Jesus through the power of His Spirit in you. Jesus described this spiritually organic growth process like this:

> I am the vine; you are the branches. If you remain in me and I in you, you will bear much fruit; apart from me you can do nothing. If you do not remain in me, you are like a branch that is thrown away and withers; such branches are picked up, thrown into the fire and burned. If you remain in me and my words remain in you, ask whatever you wish, and it will be done for you. This is to my Father's glory, that you bear much fruit, showing yourselves to be my disciples.
>
> John 15:5–8

You not only grow spiritually by remaining in Christ's power and obeying His commands—you have full access to the unlimited power of God! If you choose to rely on yourself, however, then you will inevitably wither and die, losing the potential to produce the fruit you were created to produce. You can see clearly and become more like Jesus, or you can allow your vision to be covered in mud and lose sight of the One who loves you most.

When you surrender your life to Christ, you allow His Spirit to dwell in your heart and plant the seed of truth. The way you keep the soil of your heart fertile is by weeding out all the worldly things that try to crowd your life. "Therefore, rid yourselves of all malice and all deceit, hypocrisy, envy, and slander of every kind," God's Word urges. As you grow and mature, you require more nourishment: "Like newborn babies, crave pure spiritual milk, so that by it you may grow up in your salvation, now that you have tasted that the Lord is good" (1 Peter 2:1–3).

God's Word explains that you are no accident: "Before I formed you in the womb I knew you, before you were born I set you apart" (Jeremiah 1:5). The psalmist also acknowledges the unique way God created you: "You made all the delicate, inner parts of my body and knit them together in my mother's womb" (Psalm 139:13 TLB). No matter what has happened in your life, God can use that soil—even the dirty, dusty, muddy soil of your past—to grow you beyond anything you can imagine. "'For I know the plans I have for you,' says the LORD. 'They are plans for good and not for disaster, to give you a future and a hope'" (Jeremiah 29:11 NLT).

Where you are in your life right now is where God's miracle is taking place. When God's miracle transforms you and changes your story, you will always see things you've never seen before. Like the man Jesus healed, you will discover that Jesus is right beside you, revealing Himself, His Spirit, and His power. And like the man who had been born blind but could now see, you will realize your only response to Christ's presence in your life is to worship.

- What are some of the most obvious or dramatic ways your story has changed since you welcomed Christ into your life? What have you already seen that was new and surprising?

- How would you describe the fruit you have been producing since encountering Jesus and inviting His Spirit into your heart? What kind of spiritual fruit has God been cultivating in you lately?

- How does knowing God created you in special and unique ways in His own image change the way you view your identity and your life's story? Why?

- How has the Holy Spirit empowered you to see things—in yourself, in life, in others—that you used to overlook or didn't see? Based on what you see spiritually, where is God leading you?

Miracle in Your Mess

Just imagine what a roller coaster of emotions the man blind since birth must have experienced that day when he encountered Jesus. That morning when he awakened in the darkness without sight, he probably assumed that day would be pretty much like every other. Perhaps he hoped those passing by would be particularly generous on a Sabbath when they saw him begging near the temple. Then something unexpected happened. A Stranger stood before him, someone unknown to him.

Then this Stranger surprised him by spitting on the ground, stooping to mix mud with His fingers and then scooping some of that mud onto the blind man's eyes. Surely, he must have wondered what was going on! Was this Man trying to harm him—or heal him? Told by this Mud-Maker to go wash his eyes in the Pool of Siloam, the man followed a familiar route to this well-known location. There, he splashed cool water on his face, wiping away the mud smeared across both eyes. And then everything was suddenly clear, both literally and figuratively! He could see!

While the blind man's internal response remains unknown, it's reasonable to assume he might have been confused, alarmed, afraid, concerned or frustrated during the process. After all, he had no logical reason to do what the Stranger told him to do. Yet, he obeyed. Did he dare to hope that something miraculous was happening? That he was about to see what he had never seen before?

Regardless of what he was thinking and feeling during that encounter with Jesus, this man experienced God's miracle by choosing to obey in the midst of his mess. He was willing to accept the miracle in the mud literally spread before his eyes. Then, after going through the metaphorical mud of skeptical onlookers and antagonistic Pharisees, this man affirmed his faith when Jesus revealed His identity in the man's newly sighted presence. Much to his surprise, a divine miracle blossomed out of the muddy mess.

When you believe in Christ and access His power through the Spirit, your obedience follows naturally, without question. When you experience a messy miracle through the power of God, when you open your eyes and see what you have never seen before, obedience is simple. You know He loves you and that the plans He has for you are good and filled with hope. You know He died on the cross for you so that you might be forgiven and enjoy eternal life with Him in heaven. When you wash away the mud from your miracle, you want others to see Him, too!

When you obey God by giving Him your praise and worship, by following His guidelines and commands for your life, then you want to serve Him by showing others who He is and how much He loves them, too. You want to live out your God-given purpose and lead by example even as you serve like Jesus in humility and strength. You want to be more and more like Christ.

When you experience the power of God's Spirit transforming your mess into His miracle, then you have even more to share with everyone around you. When you wash away the muddy residue of your past, you open your eyes to your new future. You want others to see what you now see, what they have never seen before. You open your eyes with the ability to lead others to the Source of your healing!

You're blessed to be a blessing!

- How is the miracle you're beginning to experience similar to what the blind man healed by Jesus experienced? What's distinctly different and unique for you?

- Do you agree that obeying God comes more naturally and effortlessly when you're walking in the Spirit by faith? Why or why not?

- What are some ways you're aware of becoming more like Jesus as you've grown in your faith? What areas still need more time and focused attention in order to follow Christ's example?

- How has experiencing God's miracle in your mess attracted the attention of others around you? How have you reflected the power of Jesus and shared God's love with them?

LOOK AGAIN

Christ followers have no other choice but to overcome. When the Holy Spirit is allowed to grow into all areas of your life, you flourish and thrive as never before. You overcome all that has held you back.

Your Mess, God's Miracle, chapter 5, page 105

By now you know that these questions and exercises are intended to help you go deeper with the material you've been covering and to apply it more directly to your life. As you become more aware of seeing what you've never seen before, you have experienced more clarity, insight and power through the Holy Spirit's presence in your life. Even when the mud of life temporarily diverts your vision, you know you have the power and grace to experience cleansing and renewed hope. When you face challenges and experience spiritual growing pains, you know that through the power of Jesus, you are more than a conqueror (Romans 8:37).

Proceed with recording your answers and responses, either here or in your journal or notebook, just as you've been doing. If you haven't caught up with reading through chapter 7 of *Your Mess, God's Miracle*, now is a good time to do so. Remember that this portion is for you to complete individually should you be participating in a group study. Take a deep breath and ask God to speak to your heart as you respond to the questions below.

See the Light

Even after you begin experiencing God's miracle in your life, you may continue struggling with your spiritual vision. You might think that after you've seen what you've never seen before and received healing for conditions doctors could not heal, you would trust God more fully. That after God has restored your marriage or brought your children out of addiction, you would know He can do anything. That after getting your new job and increased pay, you would know that nothing is impossible.

Yet experiencing a healing miracle does not necessarily erase all moments of doubt and uncertainty. You will still have times when you wonder why God isn't intervening the way you want Him to or think that He should. You will likely grow impatient occasionally, eager to go faster than God's timing seems to dictate. Other times, you will wonder why you waited so long on God when He was clearly waiting on you.

You're not alone in these temporarily lapses of faith or moments of doubt. Even one of Jesus' twelve disciples struggled to believe that his Master had actually risen from the grave. This disciple wanted proof—firsthand, eyewitness proof—that would assure him beyond any doubt that Jesus had returned from the dead. When faced with the opportunity to obtain the proof he wanted, however, this is how he responded to Jesus' invitation:

> On the evening of that first day of the week, when the disciples were together, with the doors locked for fear of the Jewish leaders, Jesus came and stood among them and said, "Peace be with you!" After he said this, he showed them his hands and side. The disciples were overjoyed when they saw the Lord.
>
> Again Jesus said, "Peace be with you! As the Father has sent me, I am sending you." And with that he breathed on them and said, "Receive the Holy Spirit. If you forgive anyone's sins, their sins are forgiven; if you do not forgive them, they are not forgiven."
>
> Now Thomas (also known as Didymus), one of the Twelve, was not with the disciples when Jesus came. So the other disciples told him, "We have seen the Lord!"
>
> But he said to them, "Unless I see the nail marks in his hands and put my finger where the nails were, and put my hand into his side, I will not believe."
>
> A week later his disciples were in the house again, and Thomas was with them. Though the doors were locked, Jesus came and stood among them and said, "Peace be with you!" Then he said to Thomas, "Put your finger here; see my hands. Reach out your hand and put it into my side. Stop doubting and believe."
>
> Thomas said to him, "My Lord and my God!"
>
> Then Jesus told him, "Because you have seen me, you have believed; blessed are those who have not seen and yet have believed."
>
> John 20:19–29

Thomas needed tangible evidence that he himself had verified before accepting the reality of Christ's resurrection. When Jesus offered such proof, though, and instructed Thomas to "stop doubting and believe," the skeptical disciple acknowledged the truth standing in front of him with an exclamation of worship: "My Lord and my God!" Jesus did not criticize or punish Thomas for doubting; He simply wanted His disciple to trust Him more, to strengthen the faith muscle that had developed during the three years they had ministered together.

Jesus offers the same loving response to you. When you're struggling, even though you know God's miracle is in your midst, know that you can rely on God's promises and walk confidently in the power of His Spirit. During such challenges, remember what God has already done for you in the past—the miraculous way He has restored your health or the health of your loved ones, the seemingly impossible times He has mended broken pieces inside your heart, the stunning occasion when His provision appeared to come out of nowhere.

God has not created you, loved you, saved you, redeemed you and healed you to abandon you now! No matter how deep your mess, you must never forget God's miracle.

- When have you most recently doubted or wrestled with uncertainty despite experiencing God's miracle in your life? What triggered your doubt or obscured your vision to see God for who He is?

- What stands out to you in the encounter between Jesus and Thomas? How does their interaction speak to what you're going through right now?

- What are some of God's miracles that you've experienced in the past? When has He healed you, answered your prayers, provided for you, protected you or done the impossible? List at least three examples below:

  1)

  2)

  3)

- How has God verified His presence and power in your life lately? When have you glimpsed the nail marks in Christ's hands or the wound in His side?

Fresh Perspective

Remembering the tangible details of how God has shown up for you in the past often dispels doubts and uncertainties. It seems likely that the blind man whom Jesus healed never thought of mud quite the same way again. In addition to the mud Jesus mixed from dirt and His own saliva, there was another element involved in healing the blind man: water.

You may be tempted to take the importance of water for granted, but its significance, in the blind man's life and in your own, cannot be ignored. You need to be hydrated to sustain your body's health. You need water to irrigate plants and crops for food and to keep animals healthy as well. But water also serves another indispensable function. Simply put, when it comes to cleanliness, water is essential.

Washing your body, along with your home and surroundings, with water provides numerous benefits to keep you healthy and thriving. Water helps eliminate dirt, grime, germs and bacteria from your skin, hair and nails. Some people enjoy the benefits that water, whether hot or cold, has on their circulation and overall physical and mental health. Others like the way chilly waters can stimulate and awaken their senses, while likely just as many enjoy the way warm waters can relax them.

Cleaning your body is not the only benefit of bathing with water, however. Throughout the pages of the Bible, water has cleansing properties that are spiritual as well as physical. Water symbolically represents receiving what's necessary for growth, maturity, refreshment and transformation to take place. In the Old Testament, Noah obeyed God and survived the Flood while Elijah endured a drought through God's provision before divine rains restored the land. In the New Testament, we find Jesus, and Peter momentarily, walking on water as well as Paul shipwrecked and washing up on the island of Malta.

And water, of course, was required for the blind man to wash away the miraculous mud Jesus had spread over his eyes. The place Jesus chose as the source of this cleansing water is significant: "Go wash in the Pool of Siloam" (John 9:7). *Siloam*, as John's account mentions, means "sent," as in the water sent forth or springing forth into this pool. This name is surely no coincidence, though, because Jesus sent this man out to complete his miracle, and the man obeyed—and came home seeing! The water springing forth to cleanse his vision symbolized the living water springing up inside him from encountering Christ.

Instead of existing as if his life were washed up, this blind man washed up and saw what he had never seen before. Keep in mind that he was born blind and had never experienced sight. But because of his willingness to obey, this man experienced God's miracle in the unlikeliest of messes. He heard the voice of Jesus telling him to go to Siloam, and he obeyed. Even if this command surprised or confused the blind man, he didn't question it. He obeyed. And he was healed!

The same is required of you. When you hear your Master's voice, it's imperative to obey His command and follow His instructions. Knowing the sound of the Shepherd's voice is vitally important if you want to experience the fulfillment of your messy miracles in life. Jesus said, "My sheep listen to my voice; I know them, and they follow me" (John 10:27). Christ clearly implies here that whoever has your ear will inevitably have your heart.

When you were young and immature, you might have been quite self-conscious about who talked to you and who didn't, what they said and how they said it and the implications of your response to them. Growing older and wiser, you have likely learned to no longer regard others as the authoritative source for how to live your life. You have become more discerning about who is allowed to speak into your life. Once you're walking in the Spirit as a follower of Jesus, you learn to guard your heart and to take your thoughts captive to Christ in order to grow closer to God and stronger in your faith.

Before you spend some time in prayer listening for the Shepherd's voice, answer the questions below and prepare your heart to be still before the Lord.

- Why do you suppose Jesus instructed the blind man to go to the Pool of Siloam and wash the mud from his eyes? Why was obedience necessary to complete the messy miracle?

- How attuned are you to the Shepherd's voice in the midst of life's messiness right now? What voices, noises and distractions do you need to eliminate to hear His voice more clearly?

- How has disobedience hindered your ability to experience God's miracle in the midst of your mess? What is God asking you to do before you can continue to see what you've never seen before?

- When have you listened to voices other than God's and allowed them to influence your life? What were the consequences of allowing others' voices into your heart and mind?

Spend a few moments centering yourself before God and preparing to pray and to listen. Try to clear your thoughts of any distractions or preoccupying concerns. Turn off your phone and close your computer or tablet, then begin sharing your heart with the Lover of your soul.

Watch Where You're Going

You don't need mud or water or even spit to remind you of the irreversible change that has taken place in your life. You have the gift of the Holy Spirit. And when you receive the Holy Spirit, you enter into a divine friendship unlike any other.

Before His death and resurrection, Jesus revealed to His followers, "I will ask the Father, and he will give you another Advocate, who will never leave you. He is the Holy Spirit, who leads into all truth" (John 14:16–17 NLT). *Advocate* here is translated from the Greek *parakaleo*, or *paraclete*, which also means "counselor," "friend" and "helper." In fact, the term literally refers to someone called alongside to help you carry something heavy, such as a log. God's Spirit has come alongside you to help lighten your load and strengthen your faith.

With the Holy Spirit in you and with you and alongside you, you are never alone. He guides you, knows you, comforts you and reveals God's will to you. He empowers you and enlightens you. He restores your sight when you're temporarily blinded by circumstances, emotions or temptations. The Holy Spirit does all these things and so much more.

Without a doubt, the most powerful Spirit on our planet today is still the Holy Spirit of almighty God, the Comforter, the Advocate, the Paraclete! God's Word assures us that where the Spirit of God is present, there is power (Acts 1:8) and "where the Spirit of the Lord is, there is freedom" (2 Corinthians 3:17). Your miracle out of life's mess is not due to your power or anyone else's—God makes it clear that it is "'not by might nor by power, but by My Spirit,' says the LORD" (Zechariah 4:6 NKJV).

Nothing can stop the power of the Holy Spirit unleashed in your life!

- Throughout the New Testament, the Holy Spirit is described as a wind, as a flame, as Someone who comes alongside you to help carry your heavy load. To what would you compare the Holy Spirit, based on your experience with Him?

- When was the last time you needed the aid of the Holy Spirit to overcome an obstacle and you experienced His power? How did He make a way for you?

- How would you describe the freedom you've experienced since inviting the Holy Spirit into your life? What bonds and strongholds in your life have been broken through the power of God's Spirit?

- What are you presently expecting and trusting God to do in your life through the power of the Holy Spirit?

Seeing Who You Are in Christ

Throughout time and history, human beings have often struggled with living in the tension of who they are versus who they want to be—and how they want to be seen by others.

But as Jesus' encounter with the blind man reminds us, once we experience His presence in our lives, our eyes are opened to the fact that we are no longer who we once were.

We are new creatures in Christ!

Your Mess, God's Miracle, chapter 9, page 176

Neither height nor depth, nor anything else in all creation, will be able to separate us from the love of God that is in Christ Jesus our Lord.

Romans 8:39

Open Your Eyes

As you experience God's miracle in your mess, there's also the tension of the transition between the old you and the new you, the blind you and the healed you, who sees more clearly than ever. The old you, the messy you, remains mired in the past, trying to blind you to the truth and leave you flailing as the broken you, the fallen you, the sinful you, the fleshly you, the depressed and anxious you, the cursed you, the empty you, the victim you, the dead you.

In your previous spiritual blindness, the old you likely survived but never thrived. The old you was touched but not transformed, glimpsing God from a distance but not up close and personal. This old you might have struggled in religious systems but lacked intimacy with the Holy Spirit. This old you feels vulnerable and weak, powerless at times to resist temptation, to get back up and to move forward.

The new you, however, sees the truth and knows who you really are. The new you views your identity the way God sees you, as the forgiven you; the born-again you; the saved you; the delivered you; the baptized you; the healed you; the bought-and-redeemed you; the blessed, favored, and anointed you. With open eyes and an open heart, this you knows who you are in Christ: the blood-washed, Jesus-following, Bible-based, Spirit-filled, loved-by-the-Father, devil-rebuking, temptation-resisting, righteousness-pursuing you. Through the power of Christ and your relationship with His Spirit, you are now the chosen you, the prophetic you, the conquering you, the ruling-and-reigning you, the sanctified you, the thriving-and-growing, glorious you.

As the reality of God's miracle in your mess unfolds in your life, you must remember what is true about you.

The old you is dead and buried.

The old you will never come back!

You are not who you used to be—no matter how you feel or what your circumstances may be. The old you died with Jesus and has now been reborn through the power of His resurrection. In Jesus, through Jesus, with Jesus, because of Jesus, *the new you is alive and well!* Consider the contrast Paul made: "If the old way, which brings condemnation, was glorious, how much more glorious is the new way, which makes us right with God! In fact, that first glory was not glorious at all compared with the overwhelming glory of the new way" (2 Corinthians 3:9–10 NLT).

Throughout the Bible, the men and women who knew God went through a similar transition. Abram became Abraham but still struggled to believe the promise God made to him until he held his newborn son, Isaac, in his old, withered hands. Jacob believed his divine destiny lay before him but felt driven to make it happen sooner than later, eventually wrestling with God until he became Israel, the patriarch of a nation filled with God's chosen people. Naomi and Ruth, both impoverished widows, returned to Naomi's homeland, where they each discovered who God had created them to be. Similarly, the old Moses died in the desert of disappointment while the new Moses rose on top of the Mount of Transfiguration.

In the New Testament, you find the same kind of shift from who someone used to be into who God made them to be. The old Peter fell in the water and later denied Jesus three times, but the new Peter came out of the Upper Room, stood up and started to prophesy and changed the world. The old Saul persecuted those who followed Jesus Christ, while the new Paul preached the Gospel of Jesus Christ to anyone and everyone.

> Like all of them and countless other believers, you are no longer who you once were.
> While the old you glimpsed the promise, the new you will possess it.
> While the old you complained, the new you will conquer.
> While the old you hoped for glory, the new you will see God's glory!

You are no longer the you mired in the mess, blind and unable to see who you are and where you're going. You are in a new day, a new season, with a new song. God declares, "See I am doing a new thing! Now it springs up; do you not perceive it?" (Isaiah 43:19). God promises, "Therefore, if anyone is in Christ, the new creation has come: The old has gone, the new is here!" (2 Corinthians 5:17). God assures you, "Being confident of this, that he who began a good work in you will carry it on to completion until the day of Christ Jesus" (Philippians 1:6).

It's time to open your eyes to who you are in Christ Jesus!

- How would you describe the old you before you met Christ and began experiencing the power of His miracle in your mess?

- How would you describe the new you now that you're experiencing the power of the Holy Spirit in your miracle?

Focus Your Vision

Sometimes you may feel stuck in the transition from your mess to your miracle because God's method doesn't seem to make sense. Perhaps you expected a quick and immediate healing only to realize that God's miracle for you requires getting muddy, obeying His instructions and washing away the grime. You might not understand what and when and how God is doing what He's doing, so you step away from Him, ignoring the power of the Holy Spirit available to you. It might be that you've experienced so much so fast that you're afraid to keep going, anxious about the uncertain and unfamiliar terrain ahead of you.

Most likely the man blind from birth experienced some of these tensions during his transition into the miracle Jesus had for him. And you can see this same hesitancy, this same trepidation, in another person Jesus healed. Instead of being impaired by lack of sight, this man had lost the use of his legs for 38 years. Read his encounter with Christ below and underline or circle the words and phrases that stand out for you personally.

Some time later, Jesus went up to Jerusalem for one of the Jewish festivals. Now there is in Jerusalem near the Sheep Gate a pool, which in Aramaic is called Bethesda and which is surrounded by five covered colonnades. Here a great number of disabled people used to lie—the blind, the lame, the paralyzed. One who was there had been an invalid for thirty-eight years. When Jesus saw him lying there and learned that he had been in this condition for a long time, he asked him, "Do you want to get well?"

109

"Sir," the invalid replied, "I have no one to help me into the pool when the water is stirred. While I am trying to get in, someone else goes down ahead of me."

Then Jesus said to him, "Get up! Pick up your mat and walk." At once the man was cured; he picked up his mat and walked.

The day on which this took place was a Sabbath, and so the Jewish leaders said to the man who had been healed, "It is the Sabbath; the law forbids you to carry your mat."

But he replied, "The man who made me well said to me, 'Pick up your mat and walk.'"

So they asked him, "Who is this fellow who told you to pick it up and walk?"

The man who was healed had no idea who it was, for Jesus had slipped away into the crowd that was there.

Later Jesus found him at the temple and said to him, "See, you are well again. Stop sinning or something worse may happen to you." The man went away and told the Jewish leaders that it was Jesus who had made him well.

John 5:1–15

- What similarities do you see between the way Jesus healed the blind man and the way He healed the lame man? What strikes you as distinctly different about their encounters?

- Why do you suppose Jesus would ask the lame man such an obvious question as "Do you want to get well?" Why is it important for you to answer this question before you can step into your miracle?

- While Jesus did not use mud to heal the lame man, He did instruct this man to do something as part of the process of his healing—what was it? Why is obedience always a part of experiencing God's miracle in your mess?

- What words or phrases did you circle or underline in this passage? Why do they resonate with you right now?

Seeing Is Believing

When seeing is believing, believing becomes worship.

In Jesus' encounter with the man blind since birth, the essential catalyst for experiencing God's miracle in his mess was faith. It required faith for the blind man to remain silent as a stranger proceeded to spit, mix mud on the ground and spread the earthy mess over his eyes. It took faith to go wash in the Pool of Siloam, the kind of faith that didn't question or resist such an unorthodox method for making a miracle. It took faith for the blind man to obey without requiring an explanation, justification or guarantee.

This man received God's miracle in his mess because he had faith in something and Someone greater than what he could or couldn't see. This man received the gift of sight he had not expected to experience and recognized the power of God at work even before he learned Jesus' name. This man yielded his assumptions and expectations in order to move forward into his miracle rather than remaining mired in his mess, in his mind or in his misperceptions.

When it was finally time for the big reveal, Jesus asked the man He had healed if he believed in the Son of Man. The man replied, "Who is he, sir? I want to believe in him." Not coincidentally, Jesus then disclosed His identity by appealing directly to the man's senses: "You have seen him, and he is speaking to you!" This man, who had been blind since birth, who had relied on what he could hear so acutely in darkness, could now see the Benefactor of his blessing along with hearing Christ's voice. And seeing and hearing was more than enough evidence, because the man didn't hesitate to affirm, "Yes, Lord, I believe!" (John 9:35–38 NLT).

Aware of the identity of Christ, this man transitioned from "I want to believe" to "I believe!" without hesitating. In the presence of such miraculous power, he knew worship was the only appropriate response. He experienced physical sight and then spiritual sight in the presence of Jesus.

To choose otherwise, to remain blind and mired in your mess, means that you act like the Pharisees. Instead of worshiping Jesus, they overheard the exchange between Him and the miracle man and asked, "Does that mean you're calling us blind?" (John 9:40 MSG). There's a sense of shock and self-righteous indignation in their question. Which likely made them all the more resistant to the truth in Jesus' response: "If you were really blind, you would be blameless, but since you claim to see everything so well, you're accountable for every fault and failure" (John 9:41 MSG).

These unrepentant religious leaders saw only what they wanted to see—a threat to their power whom they feared and hated. They refused to look again and open their eyes. They remained blind while the man who had been born blind was granted double vision! He received the gift of healthy eyes and the gift of faith in the Giver of that gift.

This man then worshiped Jesus with love, praise and gratitude—probably with an intense and passionate joy for all he had received that day. This man knew when to stand up—before the Pharisees—and when to bow down—before Christ the Lord. This man learned to open his eyes and see, and who he saw caused him to worship. This man no longer cared what the Pharisees thought of him or what they might do to him. All he cared about was worshiping Jesus!

When you experience the power, peace and joy in your messy miracle, you open your eyes and worship just as this man did. You worship in the midst of your wounds, you rejoice in the midst of your ruckus and you praise through your problems. You sing in the desert because you know you will dance in the Promised Land. With the psalmist, you proclaim, "Oh come, let us worship and bow down; let us kneel before the LORD our Maker" (Psalm 95:6 NKJV).

- How would you describe your transition into the fullness of God's power, presence and purpose in your life? To what would you compare it?

- Have you made the shift from "I want to believe" to "Yes, Lord, I believe!"? What continues to hold you back?

- What remains for you to surrender, acknowledge Christ's presence in your life and worship Him?

- Think back on where you were mentally, emotionally and spiritually when you began this study. Considering where you are now, what has been the greatest change or shift in you?

Miracle in Your Mess

In session 1 of this study, you took a moment, closed your eyes and sat in darkness. You considered the way blindness can be both physical and spiritual. You reflected on the miracle the blind man received as he washed the muddy mask from his eyes in the Pool of Siloam.

As you've seen in Jesus' encounter with the man blind since birth, those with sight, like the Pharisees, can still be blind to what matters most, to the presence of Christ in their midst. And the blind man who began that day like any other, assuming the rest of his life would be no different, experienced healing in body and spirit as his earthly mess became a showcase for God's miracle.

You have likely experienced a similar eye-opening encounter with Jesus as He continues to reveal His power in your life. Considering where you were with God before beginning this study, take a few minutes and think about what has changed as well as the areas of your life where you would like to experience more change. Use the questions and prompts below to help you think through how far you've come and the next steps God wants you to take.

- How would you describe your experience completing this study and entering into the encounter between Jesus and the blind man? What will stay with you as you move forward?

- What has surprised you the most about your experience, whether in a group or as an individual completing this study? What has unsettled, disappointed or challenged you the most?

Remember, even though the Holy Spirit is actively working in your heart and all areas of your life, you will continue to need patience as you persevere. Consider once again the wisdom in Paul's observation: "Now we see things imperfectly, like puzzling reflections in a mirror, but then we will see everything with perfect clarity. All that I know now is partial and incomplete, but then I will know everything completely, just as God now knows me completely" (1 Corinthians 13:12 NLT).

As you move toward completing this final session, consider how you want to proceed and where God might be leading you next. Think about specific next steps that can help you keep your spiritual eyes open and clean, clear and focused on Jesus. Use these questions to assist you in seeking the Lord's direction and in setting goals for your ongoing journey.

- Considering all you've felt and thought and processed while completing this study, what stands out the most to you? What's your main takeaway?

- As you look ahead at next steps, what can you do to continue your momentum as you grow closer to God and stronger in your faith? What do you need to surrender or stop doing in order to continue seeing clearly?

- Finally, look back at your responses in session 1 and the expectations you had when beginning this study. How have your expectations been met? Which ones continue to linger?

LOOK AGAIN

It is not that God is not willing to accept you right where you are—because He absolutely is. But He wants more for you than you can see for yourself at first. Your Creator wants you to thrive and flourish, to grow and blossom in order to bring to life all that He has placed within you.

Your Mess, God's Miracle, chapter 9, page 183

As you conclude this study, you may be wondering how to take what you've learned and processed and apply it directly to your life. This final "Look Again" section is designed to help you do just that, to look ahead and make that application. If you haven't finished reading *Your Mess, God's Miracle*, now is the time.

Before diving into the questions and exercises below, spend a few minutes in prayer asking God to give you wisdom and discernment about what to focus on and how to use everything you're learning. Remember that not all questions or sections may resonate, so feel free to focus on the ones that appeal to you the most. At this juncture, some points will seem more personally relevant than others, so allow the Holy Spirit to guide you.

See the Light

While your circumstances likely vary and your limitations may not be the same as those of the man blind since birth, you face the same choices he made that day Jesus stood before him. Like that man born into darkness, you can choose to accept, obey and receive God's miracle in your mess. Or you can focus the eyes of your heart downward and backward, into the shadows of your past. You can cling to the old you and your old ways of seeing yourself and dealing with life, or you can allow God's Spirit to wash your eyes with cleansing clarity.

Your eyes can remain horizontally focused on today, or your vision can vertically align with God's eternal perspective. Either way, the direction of your vision will determine your focus. Like so many people, you can

117

experience life based mostly on the sensory data collected by your human senses and collated by your neurological capacity. You can rely on your intellect to process and proceed based on what appears to be true. But living like this will keep you in darkness, stationary and stagnant, flat and one-dimensional, blinded to the life-giving power of the living God that's available to you. Without the hope of Christ, without the love of the Father, without the power of the Holy Spirit, there is no messy miracle—there's only a mess.

On the other hand, you can see clearly all that God has for you. You can shift your sight from darkness to light and experience your life based on your relationship with the holy, almighty, living God through the gift of His Son, Jesus, and the power of His Spirit. You can live like the saints of Scripture, those pioneers of faith both named and unnamed, who chose to trust God more than their human senses. Like the man born blind who felt the Son of God place mud on his eyes in order that he might receive the gift of sight, you can experience the unprecedented joy of a messy miracle.

As you shift from darkness into light, from your mess into God's miracle, remember that God's Word provides spiritual truth, nourishment and power as you grow into the fullness of all God has for you. Scripture can also help you clarify your vision and enhance your perspective. With the goal of how you move forward in mind, read the following passage and then answer the questions that follow.

> I waited patiently for the LORD;
>   he turned to me and heard my cry.
> He lifted me out of the slimy pit,
>   out of the mud and mire;
> he set my feet on a rock
>   and gave me a firm place to stand.
> He put a new song in my mouth,
>   a hymn of praise to our God.
> Many will see and fear the LORD
>   and put their trust in him.
>
> Blessed is the one
>   who trusts in the LORD,
> who does not look to the proud,
>   to those who turn aside to false gods.

Many, Lord my God,
    are the wonders you have done,
    the things you planned for us.
None can compare with you;
    were I to speak and tell of your deeds,
    they would be too many to declare.

Sacrifice and offering you did not desire—
    but my ears you have opened—
    burnt offerings and sin offerings you did not require.
Then I said, "Here I am, I have come—
    it is written about me in the scroll.
I desire to do your will, my God;
    your law is within my heart."

I proclaim your saving acts in the great assembly;
    I do not seal my lips, Lord,
    as you know.
I do not hide your righteousness in my heart;
    I speak of your faithfulness and your saving help.
I do not conceal your love and your faithfulness
    from the great assembly.

Psalm 40:1–10

- How has God lifted you out of the dark pit of your past? How does spiritual clarity provide wisdom for walking by faith on firm ground?

- How would you describe the new song God has given you in light of the miracle He's making from your mess? What kind of song is your soul singing right now?

- Where are you looking right now with the eyes of your heart? Are you looking upward or downward, inward or outward?

- What stands out or speaks to you most directly in this passage? What impact does it have on how you move forward?

Fresh Perspective

If you want to live by faith and open your eyes to eternity, then you must continue to focus on who you are in Christ. Gazing into His eyes and following

His example, you begin to see other people with a deeper compassion, an active concern and a divine kindness. You look beyond your momentary problems and temporary obstacles and look ahead at eternal solutions. Seeing with spiritual clarity through the power of the Holy Spirit, you see through the schemes of the enemy and keep your eyes fixed on the Author and Finisher of your faith.

When you open your eyes to eternity, you realize you are part of a cause so much bigger than yourself. Like the saints before you, now you see that earth is not your home and that its pleasures are not your goal. When you live by spiritual faith and not by physical sight, you discover that loving, pleasing and serving God is all you desire. "You are coming to Christ, who is the living cornerstone of God's temple. He was rejected by people, but he was chosen by God for great honor. And you are living stones that God is building into his spiritual temple. What's more, you are his holy priests" (1 Peter 2:4–5 NLT).

You are holy not because of what your eyes see, but because of how your heart sees.

You are holy not because of what you do, but because of who Christ is.

You are holy not because of your actions, but because of the Spirit's presence.

As you reflect God's glory, you receive the fullness of His power and boldly declare:

> Whatever you put in front of me, I will deal with it!
> If you put a wall in front of me, I will shout it down.
> If you put a giant in front of me, I will stone him down.
> If you put a mountain in front of me, I will move it out.
> If you put a river in front of me, I will cross it.
> If you hate me, I will love you.
> Curse me and I will bless you.
> Kill me and I will rise again.
> Break me and I will be healed.
> Because I have the power of the living God at work in my life![1]

- What temporary obstacles continue to obscure your vision? How can you look beyond them and walk by faith, not by physical sight?

- When have you glimpsed God's power at work in your life most recently? What evidence of His miracle continues to emerge from life's messes?

- How has your view of other people and your relationships with them changed since beginning this study? Why?

- What does it mean for you to have the power of the living God at work in your life at this very moment? What is God empowering you to overcome?

Spend a few minutes in prayer praising God for the peace, joy, power and purpose you're experiencing in your life moving forward. Let Him know how much you love Him and want to grow closer to Him as you serve His Kingdom and reflect His glory.

Watch Where You're Going

As you reach the end of this study, pause for a moment and assess all that you've learned and all that has changed in the way you see yourself, your life and your relationship with God. Look back through the previous sessions, and try to determine the most important idea or truth you've taken away from each one. If you've underlined words and sentences or made notes in *Your Mess, God's Miracle*, review them as well and consider how they speak to you now. Finally, use the following questions to help you sustain your vision for experiencing God's power in all areas of your life.

- Looking back through all the past sessions, what stands out to you now? Are there consistent themes or threads you see running throughout your experiences in the six sessions?

- How has your view of God changed over the course of this study? Where do you see evidence of this change in your notes, answers and written reflections? In the way you pray and relate to Him each day?

- What passages or verses from the Bible have empowered you the most in the course of this study? Why? How do these truths help you see with greater spiritual clarity?

- Imagining your life one year from now, what do you see? How will God's miracle continue to transform your mess?

Notes

Session One Seeing Your Blind Spots

1. *Merriam-Webster*, s.v. "Blind Spot," accessed February 8, 2023, https://www.merriam-webster.com/dictionary/blind%20spot.

Session Two Seeing the Power of Jesus

1. Ohio State University, "This Is Your Brain Detecting Patterns," ScienceDaily.com, May 31, 2018, https://www.sciencedaily.com/releases/2018/05/180531114642.htm.

2. Gretchen Rubin, *Outer Order, Inner Calm: Declutter and Organize to Make More Room for Happiness* (New York: Harmony Books, 2019), xviii.

Session Six Seeing Who You Are in Christ

1. Samuel Rodriguez, *Your Mess, God's Miracle: The Process Is Temporary, the Promise Is Permanent* (Minneapolis, MN: Chosen Books, 2023), 209.

Samuel Rodriguez is president of the National Hispanic Christian Leadership Conference (NHCLC), the world's largest Hispanic Christian organization, with more than 42,000 U.S. churches and many additional churches spread throughout the Spanish-speaking diaspora.

Rodriguez stands recognized by CNN, Fox News, Univision and Telemundo as America's most influential Latino/Hispanic faith leader. *Charisma* magazine named him one of the forty leaders who changed the world. The *Wall Street Journal* named him one of the top twelve Latino leaders, and he was the only faith leader on that list. He has been named among the "Top 100 Christian Leaders in America" (*Newsmax* 2018) and nominated as one of the "100 Most Influential People in the World" (*Time* 2013). Rodriguez is regularly featured on CNN, Fox News, Univision, PBS, *Christianity Today*, the *New York Times*, the *Wall Street Journal* and many others.

Rodriguez was the first Latino to deliver the keynote address at the annual Martin Luther King Jr. Commemorative Service at Ebenezer Baptist Church, and he is a recipient of the Martin Luther King Jr. Leadership Award presented by the Congress of Racial Equality.

Rodriguez advised former American presidents Bush, Obama and Trump, and he frequently consults with Congress regarding advancing immigration and criminal justice reform as well as religious freedom and pro-life initiatives. By the grace of God, Reverend Samuel Rodriguez is one of the few individuals to have participated in the inauguration ceremonies of two different presidents representing both political parties.

In January 2009, Pastor Sam read from the gospel of Luke for Mr. Obama's inaugural morning service at Saint John's Episcopal Church. On January 20, 2017, at Mr. Trump's inauguration, with more than one billion people watching from around the world, Pastor Sam became the first Latino evangelical to participate in a U.S. presidential inaugural ceremony, reading from Matthew 5 and concluding with "in Jesus' name!" In April 2020, Reverend

Rodriguez was appointed to the National Coronavirus Recovery Commission to offer specialized experience and expertise in crisis mitigation and recovery to help national, state and local leaders guide America through the COVID-19 pandemic.

Rodriguez is the executive producer of two films: *Breakthrough*, the GMA Dove Award winner for Inspirational Film of the Year, with an Academy Award nomination for Best Original Song, and *Flamin' Hot*, in partnership with Franklin Entertainment and 20th Century Fox. He is also co-founder of TBN Salsa, an international Christian-based broadcast television network, and he is the author of *You Are Next*, *Shake Free*, *Be Light*—a number-one *L.A. Times* bestseller—and *From Survive to Thrive*, a number-one Amazon bestseller.

He earned his master's degree from Lehigh University and has received honorary doctorates from Northwest, William Jessup and Baptist University of the Americas.

Rodriguez serves as the senior pastor of New Season Church, one of America's fastest-growing megachurches and number thirteen on Newsmax's Top 50 megachurches in America, with campuses in Los Angeles and Sacramento, California, where he resides with his wife, Eva, and their three children.

For more information, please visit:

www.PastorSam.com

RevSamuelRodriguez

@pastorsamuelrodriguez

@nhclc